SOMETHING HAPPENS WHEN CHURCHES PRAY

by Warren W. Wiersbe
General Director
Back to the Bible Broadcast

A
BACK TO THE BIBLE
PUBLICATION

D1023138

Back to the Bible

Lincoln, Nebraska 68501

65,000 printed to date—1984
(5-2950—65M—74)
ISBN 0-8474-6510-1

All Scripture quotations are from *The New Scofield Reference Bible* unless otherwise noted.

Printed in the United States of America

Contents

Introduction

There is a growing conviction among God's people that God is calling His Church to pray and that He has great blessings in store if only we will heed His call.

We are powerless without prayer. Jesus said, "Without me ye can do nothing" (John 15:5). Prayer ought to be our number one personal and congregational priority.

With this burden in mind I prepared these messages and then presented them over our Back to the Bible international radio network. The original messages were transcribed and then edited for publication, which accounts for occasional repetitions. We have tried to retain the "flavor" of the spoken word, even though it meant sacrificing some "literary polish."

Our prayer is that God will use these messages to stir all of us to seek God's face and pray.

> "If my people, who are called by my name, shall humble themselves, and pray, and seek my face, and turn from their wicked ways, then will I hear from heaven, and will forgive their sin, and will heal their land" (II Chron. 7:14).

—Warren W. Wiersbe

Chapter 1

Christ's Ascension—The Basis for Prayer

The Acts of the Apostles is really the acts of Jesus Christ through His Church and by His Holy Spirit. Luke began the story in the Gospel of Luke and then continued it in what we call the Acts of the Apostles.

"The former treatise have I made, O Theophilus, of all that Jesus began both to do and to teach, until the day in which he was taken up, after he, through the Holy Spirit, had given commandments unto the apostles whom he had chosen" (Acts 1:1,2). When our Lord was here on earth, He *began* to do and to teach. After He left this earth and went back to heaven, He *continued* to do and to teach through His Body, the Church.

The incredible thing is that the first Christians, who made up the first church, accomplished so very much with so very little. Stop and think what the average church depends on today. For example, we depend on organization. Some churches think that if they don't revise the bylaws and the constitution at least once a year, God can't do anything. The early church had no constitution. They built their organization as they went along, and yet God used them in a remarkable way.

7

We depend on trained leadership. I believe in trained leadership. I have taught in a Bible school and seminary, and I thank God for the training I received in schools. But the apostles were "unlearned and ignorant men" (4:13). That means they had not graduated from the accepted rabbinical schools. The early church did not have the kind of trained leadership that we would demand today, and yet see what the church accomplished.

Think about finances. Many churches feel they cannot do anything unless they have a huge budget or very generous donors. Peter said, "Silver and gold have I none" (3:6). They got together as Christians and shared what they had so that no believer would have any need.

Some Christians today feel that the church must have political power. There certainly is nothing wrong with dedicated Christians getting involved in government. But woe unto that church or that organization that depends on the government for its success! The early Christians had no political power. In fact, they were political enemies of the government. They were arrested. They were beaten. They were persecuted. They were hounded from place to place—and yet see what they accomplished!

The early church did not have the kind of organization or buildings or budgets or trained leadership or political connections that we have. So what was their secret? The Word of God, the Spirit of God and prayer. They depended on the Spirit of God. They prayed before the throne of God, and they shared the Word of God.

The Book of the Acts contains at least 30 references to prayer in many different settings. The local church rises or falls with its praying. If you ask the average member, he will say, "No, the church rises or falls with its preaching." Preaching is important. But praying was behind the apostles' preaching in the Book of the Acts. You'll find that the Apostle Paul was a man of prayer. Peter was a man of prayer. The early church believed in prayer. The local church and its ministry will rise or fall with its prayer life.

The sad thing is this: We can have "a form of godliness" (II Tim. 3:5) and yet not have any power. The machinery can be grinding, and yet nothing is coming out. There can be a great deal of activity and very little ministry. Or worse yet, there can appear to be blessings, but they don't bring glory to God—they bring glory to man. It is so sad when a local church ministry is built on a man instead of on prayer and the Word of God.

You'll notice that the Book of the Acts begins where the Gospels end—with the ascension of the Lord Jesus Christ. Our Lord Jesus was taken up from them into heaven. He went back to heaven, and then the message came to the church: "Don't stand here gazing into heaven. He is going to come again" (see Acts 1:11). It is interesting to note that everything that happens in the Book of the Acts—everything the church does to the glory of God—is based on the ascension of our Lord Jesus Christ. This helps to explain why Luke, when he wrote this book, started with the ascension. "And, when he

9

had spoken these things, while they beheld, he was taken up, and a cloud received him out of their sight" (v. 9). No wonder the Apostle Paul prayed in Ephesians 1, "The eyes of your understanding being enlightened; that ye may know what is the hope of his calling, and what the riches of the glory of his inheritance in the saints, and what is the exceeding greatness of his power toward us who believe, according to the working of his mighty power, which he wrought in Christ, when he raised him from the dead, and set him at his own right hand in the heavenly places, far above all principality, and power, and might, and dominion, and every name that is named, not only in this age, but also in that which is to come; and hath put all things under his feet, and gave him to be the head over all things to the church, which is his body, the fullness of him that filleth all in all" (vv. 18-23). Paul was saying, "I wish you people would understand how rich you are and how powerful you are because Jesus Christ, the Head of the Church, is enthroned in glory."

The Church's Authority

Let's consider the ascension of Jesus Christ and how it relates to the ministry of the church, especially the prayer ministry of the church. Let's begin in Matthew 28 where we have Matthew's record of the ascension. The Lord Jesus Christ was about to return to the Father, and this is what we read: "Jesus came and spoke unto them, saying, All authority is given unto me in heaven and in earth. Go ye, therefore, and teach all nations, baptizing them in the name of the Father, and of the Son, and of the Holy Spirit, teaching them to observe all things whatsoever I have commanded you; and, lo, I am with you always, even unto the end of the age. Amen" (vv. 18-20).

Because the Lord Jesus Christ has gone back to heaven, the Church today has God's authority. "All authority is given unto me" (v. 18). The Gospel of Matthew is the Gospel of the King. As you read the Gospel of Matthew, you find our Lord Jesus exercising authority. When He finished the Sermon on the Mount, the people were amazed because He spoke as one having authority. He had the authority to teach the truth. When He healed people, when He cast out demons, He showed that He had authority over disease, over demons—yes, even over death. When the Lord Jesus Christ forgave sinners, His enemies were amazed. "Who is this who has the authority to forgive sins?" (see 9:1-8). Throughout the Gospel of Matthew, the emphasis is on the authority of Jesus Christ.

Our Lord Jesus is no longer on earth in His physical body. He has a glorified body, and He is enthroned in heaven. But He is working today on this earth through His spiritual Body, the Church. He is the Head of that Body, enthroned in glory. We are the members of that Body, serving Him here on earth.

What authority do we have to say what we say? What authority do we have to do what we do? What authority does a pastor have to stand in the pulpit and preach the Word of God? This authority comes

11

from the Head of the Church—the Lord Jesus Christ. I've noticed three universals in Matthew 28:18-20: "all authority" (v. 18), "all nations" (v. 19) and "always" (v. 20). Jesus Christ today has all authority. Because He does, we can go into all nations. If Jesus Christ were still here on earth, His ministry would be limited. But because He has gone back to heaven and sent the Holy Spirit, you and I can reach out to all nations. The Lord Jesus has been enthroned far above all, and He is with us always. If the Lord Jesus were still in a human body here on earth—a body not glorified in heaven—He would be limited. But because He has a glorified body and He has sent His Holy Spirit, He is able to be with us and His presence goes with us always. The Church's authority is based on the ascension of Jesus Christ. This includes the authority to pray.

The Church's Ministry

At the end of the Gospel of Mark we read these words: "So then, after the Lord had spoken unto them, he was received up into heaven, and sat on the right hand of God. And they went forth, and preached everywhere, the Lord working with them, and confirming the word with signs following. Amen" (16:19,20). That's a fascinating statement, isn't it? Because our Lord has been received back into heaven, we can go forth everywhere. The Lord Jesus died for the sins of the whole world. He has gone back to heaven and is enthroned in glory. Therefore, we have a message for the whole world. If you had to invent one message that would be good for the whole world, what would it be? Only one message is good for everyone in the world, the message of the Gospel—that Christ died for the sins of the world and that sinners can be saved by trusting Him.

Wherever the first believers went, the Lord worked with them. Mark 16:20 is the equivalent of Philippians 2:12,13: "Work out your own salvation with fear and trembling. For it is God who worketh in you both to will and to do of his good pleasure." The Lord worked *for* us on the cross. He works *in* us by His Spirit. He works *through* us to reach a world when we pray and obey Him. So the Church's *authority* comes from the ascension, and the Church's *ministry* comes from the ascension. We can minister to the entire world because we have a Saviour who has overcome the world.

The Church's Energy

"And he [the Lord Jesus] led them [His disciples] out as far as to Bethany; and he lifted up his hands, and blessed them. And it came to pass, while he blessed them, he was parted from them, and carried up into heaven. And they worshiped him, and returned to Jerusalem with great joy; and were continually in the temple, praising and blessing God. Amen" (Luke 24:50-53). What were they waiting for? They were waiting for the power of the Holy Spirit. "And, behold, I send the promise of my Father upon you; but tarry ye in the city of Jerusalem, until ye be endued with power from on high" (v. 49). The Church's *energy*—the power of the

13

Holy Spirit—comes because of the ascension. Luke ended his Gospel with these people waiting for the Spirit to come. Acts begins with this same group waiting for the Spirit to come, and they were waiting in prayer.

The Church's authority, the Church's ministry and the Church's energy are all based on the ascension of Jesus Christ. This brings us to Acts 1 where we find the local church meeting together in prayer. "These all continued with one accord in prayer and supplication" (v. 14). The Church's activity is based on the ascension of our Lord Jesus Christ. He went back to heaven. He promised to send the Holy Spirit. What is the link between heaven and earth? Prayer. When a Christian prays, he is claiming His authority. When a Christian prays, he is sharing in His ministry. When a Christian prays, he is receiving divine energy.

Everything we have read in Matthew, Mark and Luke comes to pass in the local church when Christians pray. The ascended Christ works in and through the local church. I don't think that most Christians really appreciate the dignity and the power of being a part of the local church. We think that Christians get together just to edify each other, just to take some notes on a sermon. Oh no, we meet together to pray because when churches pray, God does something—God works.

I am not minimizing the importance of individual prayer. I am emphasizing the power of prayer in the church. The first church meeting referred to in the Book of the Acts was a prayer meeting. I think we have reversed this. I think our priorities have gotten confused. I have noticed in my own pastoral ministry that as praying increased, we had shorter business and committee meetings. God does so many wonderful things when the church meets together to pray.

The Church's authority comes from the ascended Christ. The Church's ministry comes from the ascended Christ. The Church's energy comes from the ascended Christ. Therefore, the Church's activity ought to be praying to the ascended Christ, worshiping Him, asking Him to release His power in us so that by His authority we might be involved in His ministry.

Something happens when churches pray. Something happened in the Book of the Acts when the local church met to pray. When we pray, we lay hold of the very throne of God. When we pray, God can give us boldness, love, power and grace. When we pray, God can expand the witness of the church. When we pray, God works. Something happens when churches pray. Is anything happening in your church? Are you a person who prays? Are you a part of a prayer ministry? Churches are depending on so many other resources and neglecting the one resource that God has given to us—the marvelous resource of prayer. Yes, something happens when churches pray because the glorified, ascended Lord hears and answers prayer. Is something happening because your church is praying?

Chapter 2

Who Should Pray?

The first church meeting described in the Book of the Acts was a prayer meeting: "Then returned they unto Jerusalem from the mount called Olivet, which is from Jerusalem a sabbath day's journey. And when they were come in, they went up into an upper room, where abode Peter, and James, and John, and Andrew, Philip, and Thomas, Bartholomew, and Matthew, James, the son of Alphaeus, and Simon the Zealot, and Judas, the son of James. These all continued with one accord in prayer and supplication, with the women, and Mary, the mother of Jesus, and with his brethren" (1:12-14). This was then followed by a business meeting in which the apostles selected a new apostle to replace Judas.

About 120 people were in that upper room, and this was the nucleus of the church. These weren't the only believers in Jerusalem because, according to I Corinthians 15:6, more than 500 people saw the risen Lord at one time. But these may well have been the most important people in Jerusalem because they were doing the most important thing anybody can do—they were involved in the fellowship of prayer. The word "fellowship" means "to have in common," and it is used often in the New Testament.

Church Members Must Pray

As Christians, we have a great deal in common. We belong to the same family. We pray to the same Father. We are indwelt by the same Holy Spirit. We belong to the same spiritual Body. We have the same blessed hope—looking for the Lord Jesus to return. Many Christians use the word "fellowship" to describe sitting across the table from each other, drinking coffee and eating a piece of pie. We can have fellowship in that way, but it may not be very deep. The deepest kind of fellowship that we can have as Christians is the fellowship of prayer.

It is interesting to note in Acts 1 the variety of people involved in this prayer meeting. To begin with, both men and women were there. The women mentioned in verse 14 were those who ministered to the Lord Jesus Christ (see Luke 8:2,3). Our Lord Jesus led these women into the glorious experience of salvation, and they joined with the men in the place of prayer, sharing in the fellowship of prayer.

I notice that the apostles were also there. I notice that the brothers of our Lord Jesus were there: "And Mary, the mother of Jesus, and with his brethren" (Acts 1:14). His brothers are named in Matthew 13:55 and Mark 6:3: James and Joseph, Simon and Judas. These people were not originally believers in the Saviour. John 7:5 says, "For neither did his brethren believe in him." However, after His resurrection, they became believers. James became a leader in the early church, and Judas (or Jude) wrote the epistle that bears his name. The point I

17

am making is this: The apostles had been walking with the Lord for about three years. The Lord's brothers had just been saved a short time. And yet both groups were in the prayer meeting! So mature Christians and new converts were in the prayer meeting. I don't know why pastors don't realize that new converts need to be in prayer meetings. They need to learn how to pray.

The apostles and the common people, known and unknown people, were there. Matthew was there. He used to work *for* the Roman government. Simon the Zealot was there. He used to work *against* the Roman government. He belonged to that "commando" group that tried to overthrow the Roman Empire. Yet they were all united in prayer.

What unites God's people? It is the Spirit of prayer. I have been in prayer meetings where we were crying out to God. I never worried about what church the person next to me belonged to. He was a Christian. He was walking with the Lord, and we were bound together, united in prayer. When churches pray, it produces unity because Jesus Christ becomes the center of the fellowship. Not the pastor, not the church program, not the budget, not the building, but the Lord Jesus Christ becomes the center of the fellowship.

"They continued with one accord in prayer" (Acts 1:14). *"With one accord"* is a wonderful little statement. You find it at least six times in the Book of the Acts. In Acts 1:14, they were in one accord in *supplication.* Acts 2:1 says, "When the day of Pentecost was fully come, they were all with one accord in one place." Here they were in one accord in *anticipation*. They were waiting for the Holy Spirit to come. Acts 2:46 says, "And they, continuing daily with one accord in the temple, and breaking bread from house to house, did eat their food with gladness and singleness of heart." Here the church was in one accord in *continuation*—they continued together in serving the Lord. One accord in supplication leads to one accord in anticipation, which leads to one accord in continuation. There were no dropouts in the first church!

In Acts 4:24 we have the local church in prayer: "And when they heard that, they lifted up their voice to God with one accord, and said, Lord, thou art God." They were in one accord in *adoration*, worshiping and praising God and praying. In Acts 5:12 we read: "And by the hands of the apostles were many signs and wonders wrought among the people (and they were all with one accord in Solomon's porch)." They were in one accord in their *association*: no divisions, no backbiting, no criticizing.

Acts 15:25 contains another reference to "one accord": "It seemed good unto us, being assembled with one accord, to send chosen men unto you with our beloved Barnabas and Paul." They were in one accord in their *determination*. They were sending out messengers, bearing the results of the church conference. But it all began with one accord in prayer. One accord in supplication leads to one accord in anticipation. This leads to one accord in continuation, one accord in adoration, one accord

19

in association and one accord in determination. No wonder church members ought to be involved in praying!

Do you belong to a local church? You ought to! If you know Jesus Christ as your Saviour, you ought to be in active fellowship in a local church because that's where every Christian belongs. And you ought to be involved in some way in the prayer ministry of the local church. Your work schedule may not allow you to go to every prayer meeting, but you ought to be praying daily for your pastor and praying with and for the people of God. Church members ought to pray together.

Church Leaders Must Pray

Not only must church members pray together, but also church leaders must pray together. Acts 3:1 says, "Now Peter and John went up together into the temple at the hour of prayer, being the ninth hour." That's interesting, isn't it? They were Christians who belonged to the church, and yet they were still going to the Jewish temple, observing the Jewish hours of prayer. Is it wrong to have special places for prayer? No. Our Lord Jesus enjoyed going to the Garden of Gethsemane to pray.

Is it wrong to have special times for prayer? Of course not. In fact, if we don't have *special* times for prayer, it is likely that we are not going to be praying at any other time. The psalmist said, "Evening, and morning, and at noon, will I pray, and cry aloud, and he shall hear my voice" (Ps. 55:17). Daniel, you recall, had stated hours for prayer. "Now when

Daniel knew that the writing was signed, he went into his house; and his windows being open in his chamber toward Jerusalem, he kneeled upon his knees three times a day, and prayed, and gave thanks before his God, as he did previously" (Dan. 6:10).

Nothing is wrong with stated hours for prayer. It was the third hour of the day when the church was praying and the Holy Spirit came (Acts 2:15). That would have been 9:00 in the morning. The sixth hour is mentioned for prayer in Acts 10:9, and the ninth hour is mentioned in Acts 3:1 and Acts 10:30. It is wonderful when church leaders meet together to pray. Peter and John, two opposite kinds of people, went to pray together. Both of them were filled with the Holy Spirit of God, and together they went to the temple to pray. They had fished together (Luke 5:10). They had prepared the Passover together (22:8). They had visited the tomb together (John 20:3,4). They had witnessed together before the Jewish council (Acts 4:13). Later, they went to Samaria together to minister to the people (8:14). Here they were praying together. It is amazing that today men who fish together and play baseball together and drink coffee together cannot pray together! In the local church, church leaders need to meet for prayer.

Church Families Must Pray

Church members ought to pray, and church leaders ought to be a part of the fellowship of prayer. Church families ought to meet together for prayer. Acts 21:5 says, "When we had accomplished those days, we departed and went our way; and they all brought us on our way, with wives and children, till we were out of the city. And we knelt down on the shore, and prayed." This is one of the farewell meetings of the Apostle Paul. You find another one in Acts 20:36 when he knelt and prayed with the elders from the Ephesian church. Here we have husbands, wives and children kneeling and praying together. Church families need to pray.

VITAL I think it is important that mothers and fathers set a godly example for their children. Do your children _EXAMPLE_ see you pray? Do they know that you pray? Do they know that when you go into your "closet" and close the door, you are going to pray? You say, "Well, our children are grown and married." Do they have the memory of mother and father praying, of family prayers together? Parents need to set the example. We need to be men and women of prayer so that our children grow up to be men and women of prayer.

Prayer is necessary to protect the home. I would _PROTECTION_ not want to send my children out to school—even to a Christian school—without sheltering them and protecting them through prayer. It is marvelous when families get together—husbands and wives, parents and children—and pray together. It is important that our children learn who the missionaries are and pray for them.

Yes, church families need to pray. You say, "But our family is very busy. We go in all directions at one time." We've been through that. The older our children get the more involved they become in church and jobs and things like that. But sometime during the day, we need to get everybody together to read the Word of God and pray.

The greatest fellowship in all the world is the fellowship of prayer. Church members need to pray together—young converts as well as mature Christians, the men as well as the women, the officers as well as the regular members. The church leaders, like Peter and John, need to meet together for prayer. And certainly our families need to meet together for prayer. Something happens when churches pray because prayer produces a creative fellowship between church members and church officers and church families. And that kind of prayer fellowship changes lives to the glory of God.

Chapter 3

Prayer and the New Christian

If a person is truly born again, prayer will be as natural to him as breathing. The life of the Christian begins with prayer. "For whosoever shall call upon the name of the Lord shall be saved" (Rom. 10:13). And the life of the Christian matures through prayer. I personally believe it is impossible for anyone to be an effective, maturing Christian apart from a disciplined prayer life.

This explains why the New Testament church emphasized prayer among their new converts. When people trusted the Lord Jesus Christ, they were introduced to a fellowship of prayer. "Then they that gladly received his word were baptized; and the same day there were added unto them about three thousand souls. And they continued steadfastly in the apostles' doctrine and fellowship, and in breaking of bread, and in prayers" (Acts 2:41,42). Here we are told that the believers who were converted at Pentecost were introduced to a life of prayer.

When I was born again in 1945, one of the first things I did was participate in a prayer meeting. A group of young people had been converted, and we needed spiritual guidance. We were grateful for what the church was doing, but we needed some extra help. In those days they didn't have follow-up courses and all the things we have today. So a group of Christians got together and began a Tuesday night prayer meeting and Bible study in one of the homes. I can remember being in that prayer meeting. It was all new to me, but I learned the importance of prayer. How I thank God for those Christians who encouraged me early in my Christian life to depend on the power of prayer.

The Believers at Pentecost

I want us to consider two examples of new converts and their prayer life. In Acts 2:42 we have the believers at Pentecost, our first example of new Christians and prayer. Peter had preached the Word of God, and the unsaved people had cried out, "What shall we do?" (v. 37). He told them to call on the name of the Lord, to believe on the Lord Jesus Christ. And they did this. Peter was obeying the Great Commission. Our Lord had said, "Go out and make disciples of all the nations" (see Mark 16:15). That means win them to Christ. Then they were to baptize them and teach them (see Matt. 28:19,20). That's what Peter did. He preached the Word of God, and the people believed and were baptized. Then they were introduced into the fellowship of the local church.

In the New Testament there is no such thing as the isolated Christian. People who trusted the Lord

25

were introduced to the church fellowship and became a part of it. These people were baptized, and they continued. That's the best kind of Christian—the kind that continues! They continued *steadfastly*—not just intermittently with a little bit of enthusiasm—in the apostles' teaching. New Christians need to be taught the Word of God. The Word of God is their food and their light. It's their sword for fighting the Devil. It's water for keeping clean. They were taught the apostles' doctrine, and they participated in the apostles' fellowship.

Fellowship means more than just getting together; it means sharing. Here I think it refers to the fact that they sold their possessions and shared with each other. We don't require this of church members today, but I do believe that the word "fellowship" in Acts 2:42 is talking about stewardship, the sharing of what we have with others. Throughout the New Testament the word "fellowship" is connected with giving. You will find this in II Corinthians 8:4 and 9:13 and Philippians 1:5. When Paul wrote to the Philippian church, he was thankful for their fellowship in the Gospel. What did that mean? It meant that they had shared with him financially.

So the new Christians were introduced to Bible teaching, doctrine, fellowship, giving, breaking of bread (which probably refers to the Lord's Supper and to the everyday meals they had together as believers). It is my belief that in the early church, at the close of their everyday meals, they would take the bread and the cup and observe the Lord's Supper. Notice that Acts 2:42 climaxes with prayers. They were introduced to the importance of prayer.

When a person is born again, the Holy Spirit of God comes into his life and prayer becomes a vital part of his life. In Romans 8:15 we read: "For ye have not received the spirit of bondage again to fear; but ye have received the Spirit of adoption, whereby we cry, Abba, Father." We have a similar verse in Galatians 4:6: "And because ye are sons, God hath sent forth the Spirit of his Son into your hearts, crying, Abba, Father." When a person is born again, instinctively because of the Holy Spirit within, he speaks to the Father.

The Christian life begins with prayer. It grows with prayer. The great Baptist preacher Charles Haddon Spurgeon said, "Prayer is the autograph of the Holy Ghost upon the renewed heart." Why must new Christians be taught how to pray? For one thing, when a person is saved, there is initially that exhilaration, that enthusiasm, that wonderful feeling of freedom from bondage, and a new Christian is prone to live on that feeling. Then the Devil shows up and begins to create problems through testing and temptation. If a Christian lives on his feelings or on his fellowship with other Christians, he will fail the Lord. But if he learns how to pray, he will grow in the Lord.

Prayer acknowledges the lordship of Christ. Prayer gives evidence that we know the Father in heaven. Prayer shows that we know our own weaknesses and our own needs. Prayer gives evidence that we are trusting the Father, that we know He is

27

able. Prayer and the Word of God go together. Because we believe the Word of God, we pray; and because we pray, we better understand the Word of God.

When a new Christian learns how to pray, he learns how to set priorities, how to put first things first. I think it is very important when Christians lead others to the Lord Jesus Christ that they teach them how to pray. I think it is good when believers have prayer partners. When someone trusts the Lord Jesus Christ, the pastor (or whoever is in charge of follow-up) should assign a prayer partner. People can pray over the telephone. They can pray occasionally when they meet during the week. They can have stated times when they get together to pray. It is important that new Christians learn how to pray.

It is good that we give new Christians doctrinal teaching. Acts 2:42 says, "They continued steadfastly in the apostles' doctrine"—the apostles' teaching. It is good when we teach new Christians how to be good stewards: "The apostles' doctrine and fellowship" (v. 42). It is good when they become a part of the church family and come to the Lord's Table. You find here the two ordinances that belong to the local church. One is baptism: "Then they that gladly received his word were baptized" (v. 41). The other is the Lord's Supper: "In breaking of bread" (v. 42). *But let's not neglect prayer.* Let's teach these young babies how to cry out to the Father. If they have all Bible and no prayer, they are going to have a great deal of light and no heat. If they have all fellowship

and no prayer, they're going to live on fellowship—
they'll start leaning on other Christians. It is important in the local church that we teach new Christians how to pray.

The Apostle Paul

Our second example of prayer in the life of the
new believer is in Acts 9. Here we have the record of
the conversion of Saul of Tarsus, who became the
great Apostle Paul. When God spoke to Ananias
about going to baptize Paul, Ananias was quite sure
he did not want to go. "And there was a certain
disciple at Damascus, named Ananias; and to him
said the Lord in a vision, Ananias. And he said,
Behold, I am here, Lord. And the Lord said unto
him, Arise, and go into the street which is called
Straight, and inquire in the house of Judas for one
called Saul of Tarsus; for, behold, he prayeth"
(vv. 10,11). God had to explain to Ananias that Paul
had seen a vision, that he was expecting Ananias to
come and minister to him.

The important thing about Paul was that he was
praying. "For, behold, he prayeth" (v. 11). What a
change in Paul! He had been the great aggressive
leader; now he was a very humble follower. Paul had
been a threat to the church, but now he was very
meek and very weak. He had been blinded; now he
was fasting and praying. He was calling out to God.

I wonder what Paul was praying about? Perhaps
he was praying from the Psalms. Certainly he knew
the Old Testament Scriptures. "And call upon me in
the day of trouble; I will deliver thee, and thou shalt

29

glorify me" (Ps. 50:15). Or perhaps he was praying from Psalm 130: "Out of the depths have I cried unto thee, O Lord. Lord, hear my voice; let thine ears be attentive to the voice of my supplications" (vv. 1,2).

Many times Paul had gone into the temple to pray when he was a Pharisee. But now he realized that his pharisaical righteousness was of no avail. I wonder if the Apostle Paul was thinking about wicked Manasseh back in the Old Testament. "And when he [Manasseh] was in affliction, he besought the Lord, his God, and humbled himself greatly before the God of his fathers, and prayed unto him; and he was entreated by him, and heard his supplication" (II Chron. 33:12,13). Paul was now a humble man, praying to God.

Paul continued in a life of prayer. I have discovered in my own spiritual ministry that people grow the way they are born. If they are born in the midst of emotional excitement, that's the way they want to grow. If they are born in the midst of prayer and Bible teaching, that's the way they will grow. In the Book of the Acts and in the epistles, there are more than 55 references to prayer in the life of the Apostle Paul. He was born again in an atmosphere of prayer, and he continued that emphasis.

When Paul was in prison in Philippi, what was he doing? Praying and praising God. When you read Paul's letters, you find him teaching about prayer. In fact, Paul often asked people to pray for him. The Apostle Paul began his Christian life in an atmosphere of prayer: "Behold, he prayeth" (Acts 9:11).

It's as though God were saying to Ananias, "You don't have to be afraid of Saul of Tarsus anymore. He is now in the place of prayer. He has discovered that his own righteousness is as filthy rags. He has learned that his own religious power is meaningless. I have humbled him. I have brought him low. Behold, he is praying."

Paul had been praying and fasting for three days. The Pharisees prayed regularly. In fact, Jesus said that they stood on the corners and prayed. Fasting was nothing new to Paul. The Pharisees fasted twice a week. And yet for the first time in his life, he discovered the reality of fasting and the reality of praying. It was not just a religious ritual he went through. It was something very real and very precious to him.

What are we saying in this study? We are simply saying this: One of the evidences that a person is truly born again is the desire to pray. I believe that when the Holy Spirit of God comes into the heart, the new Christian will want to pray.

The new Christian needs to learn the importance of prayer. One of the evidences that a person is growing is his desire to spend time praying. Prayer, to the new Christian, is like breathing. It is power. It is life. When we pray, we are in touch with the throne of grace. We are saved by grace, we grow by grace, and we serve by grace. There is nothing that grace cannot accomplish in the life of the believer who will spend time praying.

My message is simply this: If you are a new Christian, learn how to pray. Find a prayer partner or two

31

in your church, and learn how to pray. Use the Word of God, and learn how to pray. If you are a Sunday school teacher, church officer or pastor, when you lead someone to Christ, get him or her involved in prayer. I really believe that one reason why God greatly used the Apostle Paul was because he was a man who knew how to pray, and this life of prayer commenced very early in his Christian walk.

Something happens when churches pray and especially when churches teach their new converts how to pray. As they pray, these new Christians mature in the Lord and become servants of God who can win others to Jesus Christ. May the Lord teach us to pray, and may we teach others how to pray to the glory of God.

Chapter 4

Prayer and God's Business

The first recorded meeting in the Book of the Acts is a prayer meeting. "These all continued with one accord in prayer and supplication, with the women, and Mary, the mother of Jesus, and with his brethren" (1:14). We have quite a mixture of people in that meeting! There are men and women, apostles and common people, new Christians as well as mature believers. Mary was in this prayer meeting. In fact, this is the last reference to Mary in the New Testament. The last thing we find her doing is praying to the exalted Lord Jesus Christ.

The second meeting recorded in the Book of the Acts is a business meeting where the group selected a successor to Judas (vv. 15-26). This business meeting was held in an atmosphere of prayer. They didn't suddenly get together and decide to choose a new apostle. No, they had been praying for several days. They had been praying for God's direction. We can't emphasize how important it is for churches to pray when it comes to making spiritual decisions.

It is rather distressing to see business meetings increase and prayer meetings decrease. It has always been my experience that as prayer meetings increase, the business meetings decrease and get shorter and shorter. Certainly, the church needs to meet together to conduct the business of the Lord. There is nothing wrong with committee work. There is nothing wrong with groups getting together to discuss problems and make decisions. Certainly, it is right for congregations to meet and to make the important decisions that relate to the ministry. But the lesson that Acts 1 teaches us is that the church, when it is going to make decisions, needs to make those decisions in an atmosphere of prayer.

When you think, for example, of calling a pastor, how carelessly some churches go about this. They have all kinds of meetings, and they gather information about what kind of pastor the people want. By the time you compile all of this information, you are going to have to look for a man who is a cross between D. L. Moody, Charles Spurgeon and the Apostle Paul! In calling a pastor, how important it is for the church to pray.

Prayer is important in selecting church officers. The believers in Jerusalem were selecting an apostle, and they were praying about it and seeking the mind of the Lord. In voting on church members, in appointing people to places of church leadership, in spending the Lord's money, in investing in missions or calling missionaries, how important it is for the local church to spend time in prayer!

When the local church prays for direction in its decisions, it is acknowledging three very vital factors that are involved in the work of the church: lordship, leadership and partnership.

Lordship

"And in those days Peter stood up in the midst of the disciples, and said (the number of names together was about an hundred and twenty), Men and brethren, this scripture must needs have been fulfilled, which the Holy Spirit, by the mouth of David, spoke before concerning Judas, who was guide to them that took Jesus" (Acts 1:15,16). Here Peter referred to the Old Testament Scriptures that mention the sin of Judas. Later he said, "It is written in the book of Psalms, Let his habitation be desolate, and let no man dwell therein; and his bishopric [overseership] let another take. Wherefore, of these men who have companied with us all the time that the Lord Jesus went in and out among us, beginning from the baptism of John unto that same day that he was taken up from us, must one be ordained to be a witness with us of his resurrection. And they appointed two, Joseph, called Barsabbas, who was surnamed Justus, and Matthias. And they prayed, and said, Thou, Lord, who knowest the hearts of all men, show which of these two thou hast chosen, that he may take part in this ministry and apostleship, from which Judas by transgression fell, that he might go to his own place. And they gave forth their lots; and the lot fell upon Matthias, and he was numbered with the eleven apostles" (vv. 20-26).

The first factor involved here is that of *lordship.* You will notice that when they prayed, they said, "Thou, Lord, who knowest the hearts of all men"

35

(v. 24). The Lord Jesus Christ is the Head of the Church. Peter was not the head of the Church. Mary was certainly not the head of the Church. The Lord Jesus Christ is the Head of the Church.

In Acts 1 you find the Lord Jesus Christ giving commandments to the apostles. Verse 2 says, "Until the day in which he was taken up, after he, through the Holy Spirit, had given commandments unto the apostles whom he had chosen." Verse 4 says, "And, being assembled together with them, commanded them that they should not depart from Jerusalem, but wait for the promise of the Father." This word translated "command" in verse 4 and "commandments" in verse 2 is a military term. It's a word that refers to a commanding officer giving orders to his soldiers, to his army. The Lord Jesus Christ is very definitely the Head of the Church. He works through the Word of God and prayer to give direction to His Church.

You will notice that it was "through the Holy Spirit" (v. 2) that He gave commandments. The Holy Spirit dwells in the Church. The Holy Spirit not only dwells in us individually, but He also dwells in the Church collectively. When the people of God assemble to worship the Son of God, then the Spirit of God is there to work and to give them wisdom. I notice that when Peter stood up, he didn't say, "I have a wonderful idea. We really ought to replace Judas." No, he got up and said, "According to the Word of God, this is what we ought to do." And he quoted from Psalm 41 and from Psalm 69 to back up his decision.

Some claim that Peter was out of place. They say that he should not have conducted this business meeting because Paul was the new apostle who should have been added. I think that interpretation is wrong. Paul made it very clear in Galatians 1 that he was never meant to be a part of the original band of disciples. He also made it clear that God had called him in His own way and in His own time.

In Luke 24:45 we read: "Then opened he their understanding, that they might understand the scriptures." The Holy Spirit of God had not yet come in great power, but the Lord Jesus had breathed on His disciples and said, "Receive ye the Holy Spirit" (John 20:22). He had opened their eyes to understand the Scriptures. The Word of God guided Peter in making this decision, and he knew what the qualification was for an apostle—he had to have seen the resurrected Christ. Peter knew that the Word of God said that Judas's place should be filled, and therefore, Peter did the right thing when he led this meeting.

The Apostle Peter was acknowledging the lordship of Jesus Christ. I appreciate the way he prayed in Acts 1:24: "Thou, Lord, who knowest the hearts of all men, show which of these two thou hast chosen." The Lord Jesus Christ had chosen 12 apostles on earth (v. 2); now He was going to choose another apostle to complete the ranks. He was still the Lord of the Church, and He is the only One who knows the human heart.

In my ministry, I have participated in many different kinds of meetings. I have been a pastor, and I am a member of a few mission boards; and we have to pray and make decisions. God is the only One who knows the heart; and because He does know the heart, He can give direction. We read this same phrase in Acts 15:8: "And God, who knoweth the hearts, bore them witness, giving them the Holy Spirit, even as he did unto us."

When we pray, we are acknowledging the lordship of Jesus Christ. The Spirit of God gives wisdom through the Word of God when we pray. You may have some decisions to make. The first thing you should do is acknowledge that Jesus is Lord. We must not make these decisions on our own. Your church committee has decisions to make. Your church board, or perhaps your whole congregation, makes decisions. You may be looking for a new pastor. You may be about to vote on a pastor. You may be considering a missionary. Seek God's mind in prayer! God knows the human heart, and God has already chosen according to His will.

The purpose of the church is not to get man's will done in heaven. The purpose of the church is to get God's will done here on earth. God's will is done here on earth when we pray. "Thy will be done in earth, as it is in heaven" (Matt. 6:10).

Our Lord Jesus said an interesting thing to His disciples when He was still on earth with them: "Verily I say unto you, Whatsoever ye shall bind on earth shall be bound in heaven; and whatsoever ye shall loose on earth shall be loosed in heaven. Again I say unto you that if two of you shall agree on earth as touching any thing that they shall ask, it shall be done for them by my Father, who is in heaven. For where two or three are gathered together in my name, there am I in the midst of them" (18:18-20).

My Greek professor in seminary told me that the verbs in verse 18 are very interesting. It reads like this: "Whatsoever you shall bind on earth *shall have already been bound* in heaven, and whatsoever you shall loose on earth *shall already have been loosed* in heaven." In other words, the church doesn't tell Jesus what to do; the Lord Jesus tells the church what to do. Decisions must be made in an atmosphere of prayer and submission. The church must seek the mind of Christ. Take time to pray, because the lordship of Jesus Christ functions in the church by the Holy Spirit when God's people pray.

Leadership

The first factor involved in the work of the church is lordship. The second is *leadership*. These believers didn't debate for a concensus. Five people didn't stand up and try to lead the meeting. Peter stood up and led the meeting. Peter wasn't the head of the Church, but he was the leader of the church at that time. Our Lord had given him this commission. In Luke 22:32 He told him to "strengthen thy brethren." In John 21, when our Lord restored Peter to his apostleship, He said, in effect, "Feed my sheep. Care for my lambs" (vv. 15-17). Peter was God's chosen leader for the church at that time.

Peter was directed by the Word of God to replace Judas. The apostles were going to witness to the 12 tribes of Israel. It was very important that the 12

39

apostles together witness to the 12 tribes of Israel. God's program was to the Jew first. "He came unto his own, and his own received him not" (John 1:11). Later, in Acts 12, James was killed, but the church did not replace him. Once that initial witness to Israel was over, there was no more need for 12 apostles to be witnessing to the 12 tribes of Israel. At Pentecost there had to be the complete number of apostles.

Prayer guides leadership. If you hold a place of leadership in your church, I hope you are a praying man or a praying woman. You might be a teenager who is a leader in your youth group. I hope you pray. Leadership is very important, and it must be bound up with lordship. This is done through prayer.

Partnership

The first factor was lordship, the second was leadership, and the third is partnership. *All* of the believers were involved in this decision. Apparently the apostles chose two men, and then the entire congregation chose one. We don't cast lots today. This is the last time in the Bible where you find any of God's people casting lots. We have the Word of God and prayer and the experience of the church to guide us.

All of the saints prayed in partnership—all of them asked for God's guidance, and all of them were a part of the decision. All of God's people have the privilege of coming into His presence. It makes no difference how many people are involved; there needs to be partnership. All of God's people should be involved in praying, and all of God's people should be involved in deciding. This doesn't mean that the whole congregation has to decide every detail of the ministry; but when it comes to appointing leaders, the congregation needs to share in praying and deciding.

After leaders were chosen, the believers prayed for them again! In Acts 6 when the first deacons were chosen, we read: "Whom they set before the apostles; and when they had prayed, they laid their hands on them" (v. 6). The church chose them and then prayed for them. In Acts 14:23 we read of the same practice: "And when they had appointed elders for them in every church, having prayed with fasting, they commended them to the Lord" (NASB). It isn't enough to pray in *choosing* our leaders; we must also pray *after* we have chosen them—that God will bless them and guide them.

In the first business meeting recorded in the Book of the Acts, we find these three factors involved— lordship, leadership and partnership. All three of these touch the ministry of prayer. When we pray, we are acknowledging the *lordship* of Christ. The preacher doesn't run the church; the deacons don't run the church. Jesus Christ is the Head of the Church. When we pray, we are acknowledging *leadership*. We are acknowledging that God has established leaders in the church, and we ask that God will give them wisdom from the Word. When we pray, we are practicing *partnership*. Each of us, as members of the local church, must pray and seek

41

the mind of Jesus Christ, the Head of the Church, to find out what He wants to do in His local body.

Something happens when churches pray. When churches pray, they are acknowledging lordship. When churches pray, they are assisting their leadership. When churches pray, they are participating in partnership. Something happens when churches pray. When they pray, God directs them to the right leaders, and then those leaders can challenge the church to go forward in the will of God. Are you a praying church member? Are you a praying leader? Are you submitted to the headship, the lordship, of Jesus Christ?

Chapter 5

The Word of God and Prayer

Acts 6:4 is a verse that the Church needs today. "But we will give ourselves continually to prayer, and to the ministry of the word." Acts 6 records an incident in the life of the early church when there was division. "In those days, when the number of the disciples was multiplied, there arose a murmuring of the Grecians against the Hebrews" (v. 1). The Greek-speaking Jews from out of the country were murmuring against the Hebrews who lived in the country because the Greek-speaking widows were neglected in the daily serving of food. The apostles were caring for the new converts, and many of those new converts were widows, who needed special help.

The Old Testament Law made it very clear that the widows and the orphans were not to be neglected. The problem was that the apostles were so busy, they were not able to fulfill their own ministry. "Then the twelve called the multitude of the disciples unto them, and said, It is not fitting that we should leave the word of God, and serve tables. Wherefore, brethren, look among you for seven men of honest report, full of the Holy Spirit and wisdom, whom we may appoint over this business. But we will give ourselves continually to prayer, and to the ministry of the word" (vv. 2-4).

You cannot separate the Word of God and prayer. If you do, you will have problems. What God has joined together, we must not put asunder. Our Lord Jesus said in John 15:7, "If ye abide in me, and my words abide in you [the Word], ye shall ask what ye will, and it shall be done unto you [prayer]." The Lord Jesus related the Word of God with prayer. "He that turneth away his ear from hearing the law, even his prayer shall be an abomination" (Prov. 28:9). In other words, if we don't pay attention to the Law of God, the Word of God, then our praying is not going to accomplish a great deal.

As you go through the Bible, you will find that God's tools for ministry are the Word of God and prayer. The Word of God gives us enlightenment. Prayer gives us enablement. When we read the Word of God, our faith is increased because faith comes through the Word of God. Then we pray, and God answers because our praying is guided by the Word of God.

The Old Testament priests, for example, had a ministry of the Word of God and prayer. "They shall teach Jacob thine ordinances, and Israel thy law; they shall put incense before thee, and whole burnt sacrifice upon thine altar" (Deut. 33:10). At the beginning of the verse we have the Word of God: "They shall teach Jacob thine ordinances, and Israel thy law." Then we have prayer: "They shall put incense before thee." The altar of golden incense stood before the veil in the tabernacle. It was a picture of prayer offered to God in heaven (see Ps. 141:1,2). The Old Testament priests were involved in the ministry of the Word of God and prayer.

When you read Exodus 32 and 33, you discover Moses had this same ministry. He would go up on the mount and would meet God and intercede for the people. Then God would give him the Word. Moses would come down and share the Word with the people. The Word of God and prayer.

Samuel had the same pattern in his ministry. First Samuel 12:23 is a familiar verse: "Moreover, as for me, God forbid that I should sin against the Lord in ceasing to pray for you; but I will teach you the good and the right way." Not only did Samuel promise to pray for the people, but he also promised to teach them the Word of God. The Word of God and prayer.

This was also true in the life of Daniel. In Daniel 9:2 we are told that Daniel "understood by books the number of the years, concerning which the word of the Lord came to Jeremiah, the prophet, that he [God] would accomplish seventy years in the desolations of Jerusalem." There is the Word of God. What did Daniel do? "And I set my face unto the Lord God, to seek by prayer and supplications, with fasting, and sackcloth, and ashes; and I prayed unto the Lord, my God" (vv. 3,4). The Word of God and prayer. Daniel did not simply study the Word of God. He also turned the Word of God into prayer.

45

Our Lord Jesus Christ had this same balance in His ministry. "And in the morning, rising up a great while before day, he went out, and departed into a solitary place, and there prayed. And Simon and they that were with him, followed after him. And when they had found him, they said unto him, All men seek for thee. And he said unto them, Let us go into the next towns, that I may preach there also; for therefore came I forth" (Mark 1:35-38). The Lord Jesus Christ had a ministry of prayer and the Word of God. The two must be balanced. When we open the Bible, God speaks to us. When we open our hearts in prayer, we speak to God.

Why is the ministry of the Word of God and prayer so important in the local church? Because of the blessings that result when you have the two balanced. What are these blessings? As we turn through the pages of the Book of the Acts, we discover what they are.

The Source of Our Wisdom

The Word of God and prayer are *the source of our wisdom*. We've already discussed Acts 1:15-26, which records how the believers elected a new apostle. How did they determine the will of God? Through the Word of God and prayer. "These all continued with one accord in prayer and supplication" (v. 14). Then in Acts 1:15 Peter applied the Word of God to their decision. They were directed by the Word and prayer.

One of the great problems today, I fear, is that local churches are being run, not by the wisdom of

God but by the wisdom of this world. First Corinthians 3:18 says, "Let no man deceive himself. If any man among you seemeth to be wise in this age, let him become a fool, that he may be wise." That verse means wise "by the standards of this present age." The wisdom that we need for leading a local church is different from that needed to run a store or a factory. Just because a person is a successful businessman doesn't mean he has the wisdom needed to direct the affairs of a church. "The wisdom of this world is foolishness with God," says I Corinthians 3:19. That doesn't mean that the church should not have good business principles or good organizational practices. It simply means that the wisdom of this world is not sufficient for determining the will of God for a local church. Where do we get this wisdom? Through the Word of God and prayer.

If you are in a place of leadership in your church but you are not spending time in the Word of God or taking time to pray, you are not going to have much to contribute. You are going to be an obstacle instead of an asset. You are going to be a stumbling block instead of a stepping-stone. Our source of wisdom is in the Word of God and prayer.

The Success of Our Witness

The Word of God and prayer will give success to our witness. At Pentecost, the 12 apostles and the other believers were commanded to reach the people of Jerusalem, Judea, Samaria and eventually the uttermost part of the earth. How could they

47

accomplish this? How could Peter, an uneducated, untrained fisherman, ever hope to reach the world with the Gospel? Yet Acts 2 tells us that he preached the Word of God and that 3000 people were saved! What was his secret? The Word of God and prayer. The church had been engaged in persistent, united, steadfast, heartfelt, sincere prayer ever since the Lord Jesus Christ had ascended to heaven. The church had gathered together for prayer day after day during those days when they were waiting for the coming of the Holy Spirit. I have preached in hundreds of churches around this world, and I've noticed that in some churches the saints gather together before the service to pray— really pray. In some churches the officers continued praying during the early part of the service, seeking God's blessing at the throne of grace. When I stepped into the pulpit, I could sense the power of God at work because people had been praying. Someone once asked Charles Haddon Spurgeon, the great British Baptist preacher, what the secret of his ministry was. Quietly he replied, "My people pray for me."

The Secret of Our Warfare

Not only are the Word of God and prayer the source of our wisdom and the success of our witness, but they are also the secret of our warfare. The apostles were arrested for preaching the Gospel of Jesus Christ, and they were brought before the Jewish council (Acts 4). They gave their witness, they were turned loose, and they went back to

48

their own company (v. 23). They lifted up their voice to God in prayer with one accord and said, "Lord, thou art God, who hast made heaven, and earth, and the sea, and all that in them is; who, by the mouth of thy servant, David, hast said, Why did the nations rage, and the peoples imagine vain things? The kings of the earth stood up, and the rulers were gathered together against the Lord, and against his Christ" (vv. 24-26). What are they doing here? They are quoting from Psalm 2. What do you have? The Word of God and prayer! When the early church met to pray, they turned the Word of God into prayer.

It takes the Word of God and prayer *together* to defeat the Devil. In Ephesians 6 Paul admonished us to put on the whole armor of God. "Wherefore, take unto you the whole armor of God, that ye may be able to withstand in the evil day, and having done all, to stand. Stand, therefore, having your loins girded about with truth, and having on the breastplate of righteousness, and your feet shod with the preparation of the gospel of peace; above all, taking the shield of faith, with which ye shall be able to quench all the fiery darts of the wicked. And take the helmet of salvation, and the sword of the Spirit, which is the word of God; praying always with all prayer and supplication in the Spirit" (vv. 13-18). Notice the combination: "Take . . . the sword of the Spirit, which is the word of God; praying always with all prayer and supplication in the Spirit" (vv. 17,18). The Word of God and prayer go together. We cannot defeat the Devil just with the

Word of God. We must also be men and women of prayer.

How did the Lord Jesus Christ defeat the Wicked One? He did it by using the Word of God and prayer. When He was in the wilderness, our Lord prayed to His Father and quoted the Word of God to Satan. Our Lord was guided and guarded by the Word of God and prayer.

By the way, you have this same image back in the Old Testament. When the Israelites were delivered from Egypt, they had a battle with the Amalekites. "Then came Amalek, and fought with Israel in Rephidim. And Moses said unto Joshua, Choose us out men, and go out, fight with Amalek: tomorrow I will stand on the top of the hill with the rod of God in mine hand. So Joshua did as Moses had said to him, and fought with Amalek: and Moses, Aaron, and Hur went up to the top of the hill. And it came to pass, when Moses held up his hand, that Israel prevailed; and when he let down his hand, Amalek prevailed" (Ex. 17:8-11). Here is another combination of the Word of God and prayer: the sword on the battlefield—the Word of God; the intercessor up on the mountain—prayer. The victory came, not because of one or the other but because of both. Moses could have been up on the mountain praying, but had there been no army on the field, there could have been no victory. On the other hand, Joshua and his soldiers could have been battling valiantly on the field, but had Moses not been on the mount praying, they could not have had the victory.

The Supply of Our Workers

If your church is going through problems and difficulties, if Satan is opposing your work and using people in your community to make things difficult, what is the solution? The Word of God and prayer. That is the source of our wisdom, the success of our witness, the secret of our warfare. It is also the supply of our workers. People say, "We need workers today." These workers will be called through the Word of God and prayer.

In Acts 13 we have a description of the church at Antioch. Verses 2 and 3 say, "As they ministered to the Lord, and fasted, the Holy Spirit said, Separate me Barnabas and Saul for the work unto which I have called them. And when they had fasted and prayed, and laid their hands on them, they sent them away." It is interesting that Barnabas and Saul were not called to the mission field at a missionary conference. They were ministering the Word of God. They were studying the Word and sharing it and helping people grow. Through the Word of God and prayer, they were called to serve the Lord and were sent to the Gentiles. It is good to have missionary conferences. We believe in them. Here in our own Missions Department we encourage churches to have missionary conferences, and we thank God for every blessing that results from such conferences. But every Sunday, every Wednesday, whenever God's people gather together, if you have the Word of God and prayer, then God can call people to serve Him.

The Strength of Our Walk

In Acts 20:32 we have another blessing that comes through the Word of God and prayer. The Apostle Paul was concluding his ministry with the Ephesian elders, and he said, "And now, brethren, I commend you to God, and to the word of his grace, which is able to build you up, and to give you an inheritance among all them who are sanctified." Again we have the Word of God and prayer. "I commend you to God [prayer], and to the word of his grace [the Word of God]." The Word of God and prayer give us strength for our walk.

How are we to be built up? What will enable us to claim our inheritance in Jesus Christ? Where can we find the ability to walk as children of the King should walk? In the Word of God and prayer! When we spend time daily in the Word of God and in prayer, when the church emphasizes the Word of God and prayer, we are built up spiritually. Churches don't just grow by addition; they grow by nutrition. That nutrition comes through the Word of God and prayer. How can God enable us to claim our inheritance and develop in the faith? Through the Word of God and prayer. This is the strength of our walk.

William Gurnall, the Puritan preacher, used to say, "When people do not mind what God speaks to them in His Word, God doth as little mind what they say to Him in prayer."

Something happens when churches pray and when they balance prayer and the Word of God.

The combination of the Word of God and prayer is the secret of the church's success for the Lord. It is the source of our wisdom, the success of our witness, the secret of our warfare, the supply of our workers, the strength of our walk. "But we will give ourselves continually to prayer, and to the ministry of the word" (6:4).

Chapter 6

Prayer and the Holy Spirit

Have you ever been in a meeting—perhaps a committee meeting—for three or four hours? Then you left the room, only to return and exclaim, "My it's stuffy in here!" The people in the room did not realize how stuffy it was because they had gotten accustomed to it. Sometimes you and I, in our church ministries, get so accustomed to the atmosphere that we don't realize how poisonous it is. In many churches the atmosphere is stuffy, dead and dull, but nobody admits it! The church needs a breath of fresh air!

When the Holy Spirit came at Pentecost, there was the sound of the rushing of a mighty wind. The wind of the Holy Spirit needs to blow in our churches today and drive away the fog and stale air. We need to open the windows of our hearts to the Holy Spirit and get a fresh breath of clean, pure heavenly oxygen to energize our souls. The Holy Spirit is pictured in the Bible as a dove. If a dove flew in to some of our meetings today, it would suffocate because of the stale air! The Holy Spirit is pictured as fire. You can't keep fire going without oxygen. It takes the wind of the Spirit and the fire of the Spirit to energize the work of God across the world. I wonder today if the air has not gotten dull and stale in many of our ministries. This explains why we are not seeing enlargements and excitement in God's work. We need to open up the windows and let the Holy Spirit work.

I'm not talking about wildfire. I'm not talking about a destructive hurricane. I'm talking about a freshness of the breath of the Spirit of God on our ministries today. How is this going to come? Through prayer. A definite relationship exists between prayer and the ministry and the Holy Spirit of God. The Holy Spirit came at Pentecost. This was the day He was supposed to arrive. This had been established from all eternity that on the Day of Pentecost the Holy Spirit would come. But the church prepared for His coming by prayer. They were praying together in one place when the Spirit of God came. They were baptized by the Spirit into one Body. They were filled with the Spirit of God, and great things began to happen.

Some groups today have gotten out of balance when it comes to the ministry of the Holy Spirit, but I am not going to allow the excesses of a fanatic to rob me of the essentials of my faith. I'm not going to let someone who has gone to extremes rob me of the true blessings of the Holy Spirit in my ministry. We need the Spirit's power today as never before!

Let's consider the relationship between prayer and the Holy Spirit from three different aspects: the historical, the doctrinal and the personal.

Historical

According to Acts 8 Philip the evangelist went down to Samaria to preach Christ, and many Samaritans were born again. When the apostles in Jerusalem heard that the Samaritans had been born again, they came to share in the blessings. "Now when the apostles who were at Jerusalem heard that Samaria had received the word of God, they sent unto them Peter and John, who, when they were come down, prayed for them, that they might receive the Holy Spirit; for as yet he was fallen upon none of them; only they were baptized in the name of the Lord Jesus. Then laid they their hands on them, and they received the Holy Spirit" (vv. 14-17).

Let's consider this passage from the historical point of view. The first ten chapters of Acts reveal the transition in God's program from Israel to the Church. In Acts 1:8 the Lord gave the plan for the outreach of the Church: "Ye shall be witnesses unto me both in Jerusalem, and in all Judaea, and in Samaria, and unto the uttermost part of the earth."

In Matthew 16:19 the Lord Jesus Christ gave the keys of the kingdom to Peter—not the keys of heaven, not the keys of hell but the keys of the kingdom. He gave Peter the privilege of opening the door of faith to the Jews (Acts 2), to the Samaritans (ch. 8) and to the Gentiles (ch. 10). The pattern today is not found in Acts 2 or in Acts 8 but in Acts 10. In Acts 2 Peter preached to the Jews. In Acts 8 he ministered to the Samaritans. In Acts 10 Peter ministered to the Gentiles, and they received the Holy Spirit when they believed. "To him give all the prophets witness, that through his name whosoever believeth in him shall receive remission of sins. While Peter yet spoke these words, the Holy Spirit fell on all them who heard the word" (vv. 43,44). They didn't have to be baptized to receive the Holy Spirit. They didn't experience the laying on of hands as the Samaritans did. Peter didn't put his hands on them or pray for them. Rather, they received the Spirit of God when they believed.

Don't build your doctrine of the Holy Spirit only on the events recorded in Acts 1—9. This is a transition period. Some people say, "Unless you have someone ordained of God lay hands on you, you can't receive the Holy Spirit." That's not true. According to Ephesians 1, you receive the Holy Spirit of God when you believe. "In whom ye also trusted, after ye heard the word of truth, the gospel of your salvation; in whom also after ye believed, ye were sealed with that Holy Spirit of promise" (v. 13). The Spirit of God enters your life when you believe on the Lord Jesus Christ.

Why did Peter and John have to go to Samaria and pray for these people that they might receive the Holy Spirit? For this reason: God was building *one* Church. The apostles had to go to Samaria in order to heal the breach that had separated the Jews and the Samaritans for centuries. The Jews had no dealings with the Samaritans; they hated each other. The Pharisees used to pray that no

Samaritan would be raised from the dead or enter into the kingdom. When Peter and John went down to Samaria and prayed for the new believers, the Samaritans who had believed received the Holy Spirit. This produced a united Church—not a Jewish church in Jerusalem and a Samaritan church in Samaria. No, there was one Body. Who created this one Body? The Holy Spirit of God. Peter was saying to these Samaritan believers, "We're not going to have a separate church for each group. We are one Body. We all belong to the Lord Jesus Christ.

This does not mean that someone today has to pray for you to receive the Holy Spirit. It is good for us to pray for one another to receive the *power* of the Spirit, the *fullness* of the Spirit. Two elderly ladies came to D. L. Moody one day and said, "We are praying for you." He said, "No, pray for the lost souls." They said, "No, we are praying for you that you might be endued with power from on high." Then Mr. Moody began to pray with these two ladies, and one day the Holy Spirit filled D. L. Moody in a remarkable way. God used him to change the lives of multitudes of people. We can pray for one another that we might receive the fullness of the Spirit, the power of the Spirit, but we do not pray for each other that we might receive *the gift* of the Spirit. The gift of the Spirit is given at conversion, when we trust Jesus Christ.

Doctrinal

Consider the doctrinal aspect of the Holy Spirit and prayer. Zechariah 12:10 helps us understand the relationship between prayer and the Spirit: "And I will pour upon the house of David, and upon the inhabitants of Jerusalem, the Spirit of grace and of supplications; and they shall look upon me whom they have pierced, and they shall mourn for him, as one mourneth for his only son." The Holy Spirit is called the "Spirit of grace and of supplications." That means the Holy Spirit of God is the Spirit of prayer. When I was born again, the Holy Spirit came into my heart and said, "Abba, Father" (Gal. 4:6). My initial response after my conversion was to look up to God and say, "Father." The Holy Spirit in the life of a new believer instills a desire for prayer. I didn't look up and say, "Judge" or "King" or "Creator." I said, "Father." The Holy Spirit is the Spirit of adoption, and the Spirit of adoption says to me, "God is your Father." (See Rom. 8:15,16.) You have an adult standing in the family of God. You may ask for what you need. You may draw upon your spiritual resources. You are an heir of God, a joint-heir with Christ.

The Holy Spirit creates the desire for prayer. If during the day, you feel a desire to pray, that's the Holy Spirit at work. Stop and pray. If you are doing something that you cannot stop, pray from your heart anyway. It is so important that during the day, when the Spirit of God speaks to us, we pause to pray. I've had the experience of being awakened in the night and having the Spirit of God burden my heart for somebody. I recall once being in Scotland. I was awakened in the night, and one of our church members came to my mind. I began to pray for her.

59

Weeks later, when I returned home, I asked her about that time and that date. She told me she was going through a very critical experience at that moment. The Lord had burdened me as her pastor to pray for her. The Spirit of God is the Spirit of prayer and supplications. He creates the desire for prayer.

Second, He also intercedes *with* us as we pray and intercedes *for* us. Romans 8:26,27 says, "Likewise, the Spirit also helpeth our infirmity; for we know not what we should pray for as we ought; but the Spirit himself maketh intercession for us with groanings which cannot be uttered. And he that searcheth the hearts knoweth what is the mind of the Spirit, because he maketh intercession for the saints according to the will of God." I don't always know the will of God. So many times people share burdens with me, but I don't know how to pray for them! But the Holy Spirit does know how to pray, and the same Holy Spirit of God who creates the desire for prayer also gives us the wisdom to know what to pray for. We can pray in the will of God if we are guided by the Holy Spirit.

The Holy Spirit of God reveals God's promises to us as we read the Word. He encourages us to claim God's promises. It is wonderful to have the Spirit of God direct you in your praying. This doesn't mean we shouldn't have a list of prayer requests. But while we are praying, we must not be limited to that list. Our praying could become routine and very legalistic. We must allow the Spirit of God to give us the freedom to pray as He directs us. I've heard

60

people say, "As I was praying, I completely lost myself." I'm afraid of that kind of experience. Why? Because the Holy Spirit of God creates the fruit of the Spirit, and part of the fruit of the Spirit is self-control. If you lose your self-control, the Holy Spirit is not at work. That's another kind of spirit! When we are praying in the Spirit, God does not bypass our mind or our heart. He uses our faculties. He reveals to us the will of God through the Word of God, and we can pray with power.

Personal

Now for a personal application. Let's answer some vital questions.

Are you born again? Do you have the witness of the Holy Spirit within, or is your praying mechanical? Does the Holy Spirit within create in you the desire to talk to your Father? Not just on Sundays or in your morning devotions but all day long? While you are working at the sink, doing the dishes, while you are doing your homework, while you are driving down the highway, even while you are ministering in the pulpit, are you led by the Spirit to pray? So many times when I've been preaching, I've been crying out to God from my heart for His power and His blessing. Can you really claim that the Holy Spirit of God within you says, "Abba, Father"?

Are you on good terms with the Holy Spirit? In Jude 1:20,21 we read: "But ye, beloved, building up yourselves on your most holy faith, praying in the Holy Spirit, keep yourselves in the love of God." Are you keeping yourself in the love of God so you

61

can pray in the Holy Spirit? Or do you just run to the Lord when you face a crisis? Do you run to ask Him for help only when you experience trouble? It is wonderful when the saints of God are not grieving the Holy Spirit, lying to the Holy Spirit or quenching the Holy Spirit. When church members get together to pray, when there is fellowship and unity, love and forgiveness, how the wind of the Holy Spirit can blow! Are you yielded so that the Holy Spirit can pray through you? You won't get any credit for this. People may not know about your praying; but God will be glorified, and one day you shall be rewarded. The machinery of the world runs on prayer. God uses the saints to pray, and through their prayers He accomplishes great things. The Holy Spirit of God worked in the Book of the Acts because people were praying and were yielded to the Spirit of God. The Spirit of God led them and taught them. The wind of the Spirit blew in their meetings and kept them from becoming stale and dull and stuffy as our meetings often become today.

Something happens when churches pray because when we pray in the Holy Spirit, He uses prayer to accomplish God's will. When we are praying in the Holy Spirit, He releases the power of God and ordinary people can do *extraordinary* things because the Spirit of God is at work. Don't say that God cannot work in your church because you don't have the buildings or because you don't have money or because you don't have exceptional talent. You have the Holy Spirit of God. You have an open access to the throne of God. When the saints of God are right with God, when our hearts are clean, when our hands are clean, when we love one another, when we pray together, the Spirit of God begins to work in and through the people of God. Something happens when churches pray because the Spirit of God uses prayer to accomplish God's will and bring God's blessing.

Chapter 7

Prayer and Government

The apostles preached the Word of God fearlessly, and as a result they were arrested and taken before the council (see Acts 4). They were threatened by the council and told not to preach any more in the name of the Lord Jesus. The reason, of course, is obvious: The council was controlled by the Sadducees, and they did not believe in the resurrection. The miracle that Peter and John performed in Acts 3 proved that Jesus Christ was alive, but the Sadducees did not want anyone to believe that Jesus was alive.

When the apostles were released, Acts 4:23,24 tells us what they did. They went back to the assembly of God's people, and they had a prayer meeting. They did not picket the council. They did not write nasty letters to their leaders. No, they turned to the living God in prayer. In the Book of the Acts, prayer is mentioned at least 30 times, and one of the truly great prayers in the Bible is in Acts 4.

"And being let go, they went to their own company, and reported all that the chief priests and elders had said unto them. And when they heard that, they lifted up their voice to God with one accord, and said, Lord, thou art God, who hast made heaven, and earth, and the sea, and all that in them is; who, by the mouth of thy servant, David, hast said, Why did the nations rage, and the peoples imagine vain things? The kings of the earth stood up, and the rulers were gathered together against the Lord, and against his Christ. For of a truth against thy holy child, Jesus [Thy holy servant, Jesus], whom thou hast anointed, both Herod, and Pontius Pilate, with the nations, and the people of Israel, were gathered together, to do whatever thy hand and thy counsel determined before to be done. And now, Lord, behold their threatenings; and grant unto thy servants, that with all boldness they may speak thy word, by stretching forth thine hand to heal; and that signs and wonders may be done by the name of thy holy child, Jesus. And when they had prayed, the place was shaken where they were assembled together; and they were all filled with the Holy Spirit, and they spoke the word of God with boldness" (vv. 23-31).

Hear Their Prayer

That is quite a prayer! Let's first of all *listen to their prayer*, and then *let's watch and see what happened because they prayed*.

I notice first of all that they prayed because they believed in God's power. "Lord, thou art God, who hast made heaven, and earth, and the sea, and all that in them is" (Acts 4:24). They prayed to God, who is the Creator of the world. All of nature looks to God for help and strength and sustenance, and we must depend on Him too.

Psalm 146 talks about the Creator: "Happy is he that hath the God of Jacob for his help, whose hope is in the Lord, his God; who made heaven, and earth, the sea, and all that therein is; who keepeth truth forever; who executeth justice for the oppressed; who giveth food to the hungry. The Lord looseth the prisoners; the Lord openeth the eyes of the blind; the Lord raiseth those who are bowed down; the Lord loveth the righteous" (vv. 5-8). When they prayed to the Lord, who made heaven and earth, they were quoting from Psalm 146. The God who created everything is the God who can take care of everything. They believed in God's power.

I wonder if they weren't also thinking about Isaiah 42:5-7: "Thus saith God, the Lord, he who created the heavens, and stretched them out; he who spread forth the earth, and that which cometh out of it; he who giveth breath unto the people upon it, and spirit to them that walk in it: I, the Lord, have called thee in righteousness, and will hold thine hand, and will keep thee, and give thee for a covenant of the people, for a light of the nations, to open blind eyes, to bring out the prisoners from the prison, and those who sit in darkness out of the prison house." The God of creation is the sovereign God. The word "Lord" in Acts 4:24 gives us our English word "despot." God is sovereign! He is the only One who can do anything for us. Do you pray to the God who is the Creator and the Sustainer, the God who has all power?

Second, I notice that, when they prayed, not only

did they believe in God's power but they relied on God's Word. They quoted from Psalm 2:1,2. "Why did the nations [the Gentiles] rage, and the peoples [the Jews] imagine vain things? The kings [Herod] of the earth stood up, and the rulers [Pilate] were gathered together against the Lord, and against his Christ" (Acts 4:25,26). They applied Psalm 2 to their specific situation. In other words, their praying was based on the Word of God. They did not separate the Word of God and prayer. "If ye abide in me, and my words abide in you, ye shall ask what ye will, and it shall be done unto you" (John 15:7).

They believed in God's power, they relied on God's Word, and they yielded to God's will: "To do whatever thy hand and thy counsel determined before to be done" (Acts 4:28). This is not fatalism. This is not just sitting back and saying, "What's going to be is going to be." This is believing that the sovereign God is accomplishing His purposes in this world. How do churches pray for the government? How do we pray for the authorities over us? We pray, "Father, accomplish Thy will in us and through us." In verse 29 they called themselves "servants," and the word means "bondsmen." They were yielded to God's will.

They prayed believing in God's power, relying on God's Word and yielded to God's will. They didn't try to overthrow the government. They didn't go and speak disrespectfully to those in places of authority. No, they prayed to the highest authority in the universe. They came to the throne of grace and said, "Lord, thou art God" (v. 24). You don't

67

hear much praying like that today. When something happens in the city council, the state government or the federal government that upsets the church, many Christians try every other means except prayer to get things changed. It isn't wrong for Christians to be involved in government, nor is it wrong for us to campaign for good laws. But it is wrong for us to trust the government instead of God. It is wrong for us to put our faith even in *Christian* politicians instead of in Christ, who is King of kings and Lord of lords.

They were burdened for God's glory. "And now, Lord, behold their threatenings; and grant unto thy servants, that with all boldness they may speak thy word, by stretching forth thine hand to heal; and that signs and wonders may be done by the name of thy holy child, Jesus" (vv. 29,30). Some people would have prayed, "Sovereign Lord, send fire from heaven to destroy these people!" They didn't pray that way. God said, "Vengeance is mine; I will repay, saith the Lord" (Rom. 12:19). They sought only to honor the name of the Lord Jesus. They didn't ask for escape; they asked for power. They didn't ask for their circumstances to change. They asked for boldness to use their circumstances for the glory of God. They did not pray for revenge. They prayed that God would be glorified.

Finally, their praying centered in God. They were not looking at themselves or at their circumstances. They were looking at God. Too often our praying centers on ourselves when it ought to focus on God.

68

We have listened to their prayer and learned how we ought to pray. Some missionaries may be having difficulties with authorities. What should you do? Do everything you can do legally—but also pray. "Go over their heads" and pray to the God of the universe, the God of creation. The God who keeps the planets from running into each other can keep His work going on this earth.

See What Happened

Let's look at the answer God gave. "And when they had prayed, the place was shaken where they were assembled together" (Acts 4:31). That doesn't happen much in our prayer meetings today. Sometimes you have to shake *the people* to wake them up when prayer meeting is over! "And they were all filled with the Holy Spirit" (v. 31). They received a new enduement of power. This was not a second Pentecost. There will not be a second Pentecost any more than there will be a second Calvary. The Spirit has already come. There is one baptism, but there are many fillings. They were filled with the Holy Spirit. Do you go home from prayer meeting filled with the Holy Spirit? They didn't have more money, more education, more prestige or easier circumstances, but they had a new enduement of power from God.

Verse 32 says, "And the multitude of those that believed were of one heart and of one soul." They had a new enjoyment of unity as well as a new enduement of power. Prayer ought to unify us. "And when they heard that, they lifted up their voice to God with one accord" (v. 24). We wouldn't have many of the divisions we have in the church today if we had more prayer meetings where people were praying, "Lord, thou art God" (v. 24). Throughout the Book of the Acts you find the saints of God in one accord.

Third, they experienced a new enablement to witness. Verse 33 says, "With great power gave the apostles witness of the resurrection of the Lord Jesus." The very thing they were told not to do they did even better because God told them to do it. They witnessed that the resurrected Christ was King of kings, Lord of lords and the Saviour of sinners. The church enjoyed a new enlargement as people were converted. The members shared what they had. Great grace was upon them all. I wonder if we see such results in our praying today—God's work being strengthened, God's name being glorified, God's enemies being silenced.

Something happens when churches pray if they believe in God's power, rely on God's Word and yield to God's will. Something happens when churches pray if they are burdened for God's glory and if their praying centers wholly in God. Yes, something happens *even to governments* when churches pray!

Chapter 8

Praying for Those in Authority

Two elements are lacking in our public worship today—the public reading of the Scriptures and public prayer for those who are in places of authority. Paul commanded Timothy, "Give attendance to reading" (I Tim. 4:13). He was referring to the public reading of the Word of God. In many churches today we have time for announcements, promotion and a lot of special music, but for some reason we don't have time for the public reading of the Word of God. About the only time the Word of God is read is when the pastor reads his text. I think it is important for our local churches to get back to the public reading of the Word of God.

Paul also told Timothy that we should pray publicly for those who are in authority. "I exhort, therefore, that first of all, supplications, prayers, intercessions, and giving of thanks, be made for all men, for kings, and for all that are in authority, that we may lead a quiet and peaceable life in all godliness and honesty. For this is good and acceptable in the sight of God, our Savior, who will have all men to be saved, and to come unto the knowledge of the truth. For there is one God, and one mediator between God and men, the man, Christ Jesus, who gave himself a ransom for all, to be testified in due time" (I Tim. 2:1-6). Praying for those in authority is commanded by God. Paul wrote that this is of number one importance in the local church. This is a commandment of God, and we had better obey. In our public worship, as well as in our private prayers, we should pray for those who are in authority. Why? Let me suggest three reasons.

For Their Sake

First of all, we must pray for them *for their sake*. They are only men—human beings who need God's help. "I exhort, therefore, that first of all [of first importance], supplications, prayers, intercessions, and giving of thanks, be made for all men" (I Tim. 2:1). Those who are in places of authority are simply people, human beings made of clay. What they are doing, they can do only with the help of God. They are simply humans who are in places of authority, men and women who are sinners, who have weaknesses, who need God's help. Quite frankly, I don't feel anyone has the right to criticize or judge someone who is in a place of authority unless he has really prayed for that person. I wonder how many of us really pray for those in authority? We must pray for them for their sake because they are simply people made in the image of God, clay vessels, chosen by God to do a certain task.

We must pray for them because they are ministers. This may surprise you, but it is true. "Let every soul be subject unto the higher powers. For there is

72

no power but of God; the powers that be are ordained of God. Whosoever, therefore, resisteth the power, resisteth the ordinance of God; and they that resist shall receive to themselves judgment [they will be arrested]. For rulers are not a terror to good works, but to the evil. Wilt thou, then, not be afraid of the power? Do that which is good and thou shalt have praise of the same; for he is the minister of God to thee for good" (Rom. 13:1-4).

Did you ever stop to think when you see a policeman going by, that he is the minister of God? When you see a picture of a president or prime minister or other leader in the newspaper, that person is the minister of God. Three times in this passage God makes it very clear that those who are in authority are God's ministers (vv. 4,6). This comes as a strange thought to some people. How could Almighty God work through unsaved people? Not many people who are in places of authority are consecrated Christians. Can God work through them? Proverbs 21:1 says He can: "The king's heart is in the hand of the Lord, like the rivers of water; he turneth it withersoever he will."

Daniel told us that God is in control of the affairs of the nations: "Daniel answered and said, Blessed be the name of God forever and ever; for wisdom and might are his, and he changeth the times and the seasons; he removeth kings, and setteth up kings; he giveth wisdom unto the wise, and knowledge to those who know understanding" (Dan. 2:20,21). In Daniel 4:17 we read: "This matter is by the decree of the watchers, and the demand by the

73

word of the holy ones, to the intent that the living may know that the Most High ruleth in the kingdom of men, and giveth it to whomsoever he will, and setteth up over it the basest of men." Sometimes God gives us the kind of leaders we really deserve! These verses tell us that God can work even through unconverted people. He worked through Cyrus. He worked through Artaxerxes. He was even able to accomplish His purpose through Pharaoh even though Pharaoh hated God. You and I have such a low view of the sovereignty of God that we don't really believe that, when we pray for people in authority, God can work. If the truth were known, we'd find out that the machinery of the world is run by prayer. That's what Andrew Murray wrote: "God rules the world by the prayers of his saints."

We must pray for those who are in authority because they are men and because they are ministers. Someone may say, "But wait just a minute, these people persecute Christians!" That's right. In Acts 4 we find the saints praying to God after they had been arrested and threatened. And how did they pray? Did they pray, "God, we pray that You will send fire from heaven and destroy these wicked people"? No. They asked God to give them power and boldness to do the work of God, to accomplish the purposes of God on this earth.

When Stephen was being stoned, how did he pray for those in authority? "Lord Jesus," he prayed, "receive my spirit. . . . Lord, lay not this sin to their charge" (7:59,60). Sometimes those who

74

cannot get what they want from the government become mean and critical. They start praying for fire from heaven to destroy all those who do not cooperate with them. That is not New Testament praying. You may not agree with the party, you may not even like the leader, but you have to respect the office because God is in charge of authority in government. And even if they persecute us, we are supposed to pray for them. Didn't Jesus teach that? "Ye have heard that it hath been said, Thou shalt love thy neighbor, and hate thine enemy; but I say unto you, Love your enemies, bless them that curse you, do good to them that hate you, and pray for them who despitefully use you, and persecute you" (Matt. 5:43,44). That's hard to do, but the Bible commands it.

In the church that you attend, does somebody stand up at least once during the public worship service and pray for those in authority? That's the way to get laws passed that ought to be passed. That's the way to have laws acted upon and godly principles established in a government.

For the Church's Sake

Second, we must pray for them *for the church's sake*. We must pray for kings and for all who are in authority "that we may lead a quiet and peaceable life in all godliness and honesty. For this is good and acceptable in the sight of God, our Savior" (I Tim. 2:2,3). We must pray for those in authority so that our circumstances might be quiet (tranquil on the outside) and so that our own hearts might be peaceable (calm on the inside). We pray so that there might be *godliness* (our relationship to God) and *honesty* (dignity, or respect, in our relationship to others). As we pray to God, something ought to happen to our character. Something ought to happen to our circumstances. If I am really praying for those in authority, I will live a respectable, honest, honorable life. If I am really praying for those in authority, I will live a godly life. If I am really praying for those in authority, I will be a peacemaker and not a troublemaker. "If it be possible, as much as lieth in you, live peaceably with all men" (Rom. 12:18). Sometimes you can't. When that happens, leave the consequences to God. We are not supposed to create problems for people. Sometimes as we live our faith, we create problems and some people don't agree with our faith. But that's something God has to take care of. Romans 12:17-19 says, "Recompense to no man evil for evil. Provide things honest in the sight of all men. If it be possible, as much as lieth in you, live peaceably with all men. Dearly beloved, avenge not yourselves but, rather, give place unto wrath; for it is written, Vengeance is mine; I will repay, saith the Lord."

I don't think it is dignifying, or honoring, to the Lord when Christians with loud mouths and mean attitudes attack officials in an unchristian way. I don't think this pleases the Lord.

For Lost Sinners' Sake

We must pray for those in authority for their sake and for the church's sake. Third, we must pray for those in authority *for the sake of lost sinners*. Why do we pray for people in authority? So that God might be able to work through government to give us the opportunity to win the lost. There are places in this world where they don't have the opportunity to witness as we do in the free world. We must pray that the authorities who are in office might be able to keep life safe and free. I could not preach over the radio were it not for the authority in Washington, D.C. Because there are laws that permit me to preach the Word of God, I can preach freely. We must pray that God will continue to keep the doors open so that we might constantly be free to pass out tracts, to preach, to publish, to witness to others.

Watchman Nee said a very wonderful thing about this. Watchman Nee was a Chinese Christian who was arrested by the Communists and spent many years in jail before he died. He said, "In relation to earthly nations and events, the supreme question to ask ourselves is always, how is the Church of God affected? This should be the direction of all our prayers with regard to world governments—not for or against one side or another, in politics or war, but for the will of God.

"If all history is in relation to the Lord's testimony, then we must know how to pray. It must be possible for British and German, Chinese and Japanese Christians to kneel together and pray together, and all say Amen. Our one appeal to God must be for a march of events that is of advantage to the testimony of his Son."*

But instead of that, we try politics, we try lobby-

77

ing, we try everything else we can to change people's minds. We do everything but pray!

Nothing is wrong with Christians serving in government and trying to exercise godly influence in the corridors of power. Daniel, Joseph and Esther served in pagan governments, and God used them. In the early church, there were people in civil authority who were Christians. What Paul was saying is this: We must, first of all, pray for those in authority. That's the important thing. After we have prayed, then we can do something about legislation and influencing those who are in office. We must pray *for their sake*, because they are just people. But they are the ministers of God, and God can use them and work through them in spite of themselves. We must pray *for the church's sake*—that we might have the right circumstances for serving God. We must pray *for the sake of lost sinners*, for if God allows governments to close the doors, then we will not be able to preach and share the Gospel with the lost.

Are you praying daily for those who are in authority? If you are not, I suggest you start. Is your church praying regularly for those who are in authority? Something happens when churches pray for those in authority, because that's when God begins to work and accomplish His purposes.

---

*Watchman Nee, *The Joyful Heart* (Wheaton, Illinois: Tyndale House Publishers, Inc., 1978. By Harry Foster, Kingsway Publications Limited, England). Used by permission.

Chapter 9

Prayer and Closed Doors

If you knew that you were scheduled to be executed the next morning, would you sleep the night before? Peter did. Acts 12 records that Peter slept soundly, even though he was guarded by 16 soldiers and had been sentenced to be executed! What made the difference? Prayer! Prayer can open doors. Prayer can overcome great problems. Prayer can set people free.

"Now about that time Herod, the king, stretched forth his hands to vex certain of the church. And he killed James, the brother of John, with the sword. And because he saw it pleased the Jews, he proceeded further to take Peter also. (Then were the days of unleavened bread.) And when he had apprehended him, he put him in prison, and delivered him to four quaternions of soldiers to keep him; intending after Easter [Passover] to bring him forth to the people. Peter, therefore, was kept in prison" (Acts 12:1-5).

If the story stopped at that point, there would have been no reason for Dr. Luke to write it. Notice the next two words—"but prayer." "Peter, there-

79

fore, was kept in prison; but prayer was made without ceasing by the church unto God for him. And when Herod would have brought him forth, the same night Peter was sleeping between two soldiers, bound with two chains; and the keepers before the door kept the prison. And, behold, an angel of the Lord came upon him, and a light shone in the prison; and he smote Peter on the side, and raised him up, saying, Arise quickly. And his chains fell off from his hands" (vv. 5-7). You will recall how the angel led Peter out of the cell and out of the prison. The doors opened for them automatically. The guards didn't stop them.

"And when he had considered the thing, he came to the house of Mary, the mother of John, whose surname was Mark, where many were gathered together praying. And as Peter knocked at the door of the gate, a maid came to hearken, named Rhoda. And when she knew Peter's voice, she opened not the gate for gladness, but ran in, and told how Peter stood before the gate. And they said unto her, Thou art mad. But she constantly affirmed that it was even so. Then they said, It is his angel. But Peter continued knocking; and when they had opened the door, and saw him, they were astonished" (vv. 12-16). God had answered prayer in a wonderful way.

The Power of Satan

In Acts 12 we see a number of different powers at work. We see first the power of Satan. "About that time Herod, the king, stretched forth his hands to vex certain of the church" (v. 1). The Devil always fights the church when the church is on the move. Charles Spurgeon used to say that Satan never kicks a dead horse. Satan knew that the church was on the move, so he attacked it.

In Acts 2 we read that 3000 people were converted to Christ. Later, another 2000 were converted. Then what happened? According to Acts 4, Satan came like a lion and had the apostles threatened. In chapter 5, Satan came like a serpent, influencing Ananias and Sapphira to infect the church with their lying and hypocrisy. If Satan can't win by persecution from the outside, he will try pollution on the inside. Then Satan came as the accuser in Acts 6. One group of widows accused the other group of widows of taking over. "We are being neglected," they said. Satan likes to get the saints to accuse one another.

Then, according to Acts 12, Satan came as a murderer. James was killed, and Peter was put into prison to be kept for execution. Never underestimate the power of Satan! The Devil uses people; but if you fight people, you are wasting your time. "We wrestle not against flesh and blood, but against principalities, against powers" (Eph. 6:12). Satan used Herod, and today Satan uses all kinds of people to attack the work of the Church. No wonder Peter wrote: "Be sober, be vigilant, because your adversary, the devil, like a roaring lion walketh about, seeking whom he may devour" (I Pet. 5:8). The church that doesn't pray is already in the hands of Satan. The church that is not alert, watching, guarding, is already in the hands of Satan. We must be alert, we must be aware. "Watch and pray" (Matt. 26:41).

The Power of a Praying Church

How does God defeat the power of the Devil? Through the power of a praying church. Why did Satan attack James and Peter? Because they were getting in his way. They were winning souls. They were Spirit-filled men who were serving God. They were leaders who had influence. Do you pray for Christian leaders? Do you pray for those who have influence? You may not always agree with them, but do you pray for them? Satan is out to destroy those who are in places of spiritual leadership.

God's power is released when God's people pray. The power of Satan was released through Herod's hands, but when you pray, God's hands go to work. Do you remember how the believers prayed in Acts 4? "To do whatever thy hand and thy counsel determined before to be done" (v. 28). The apostles were not saying, "Why is this happening?" They were saying, "Lord, You are in charge of everything. The time has come for Your hand to work!"

Compare Acts 4:30 with Acts 12:1. "Now about that time Herod, the king, stretched forth his hands to vex certain of the church" (12:1). In Acts 4:30 we read that God stretches forth His hand to do wonderful things. When does God's hand work? When God's church prays. The hand of God does not work apart from prayer. Prayer is what moves the hand of God. We tie God's hands by our unbelief. I hear church members complaining because people are not being saved, because the church isn't growing, because the bills aren't being paid. God's hand works when God's people pray.

Peter was asleep in the prison. He had such perfect peace for two reasons—the Word of God and prayer. Peter knew that he would not be killed by Herod, because the Lord Jesus had already told him that when he got to be an old man, he would be crucified (see John 21:18,19). Peter knew that Herod's threats were of no avail. Peter said, "Good night" to the guards, turned over and went to sleep, resting his head on the pillow of the promises of God. He had peace because he trusted the Word of God. "Great peace have they who love thy law, and nothing shall offend them" (Ps. 119:165). But Peter also had peace because of prayer. He had prayed, the apostles had prayed, and many people had gathered in Mary's house to pray.

Let's look at this prayer meeting. The church had gathered together in the house of Mary, the mother of John Mark. Acts 12:5 says, "Peter, therefore, was kept in prison; but prayer was made without ceasing." The word translated "without ceasing" means "strenuously, with agony." It is the same word translated "earnestly" in Luke 22:44 when the Lord Jesus prayed with great agony in the garden. This group of people was not sitting around a table eating and just casually talking. They were praying earnestly. I notice that *many* of them had gathered: "Where many were gathered together praying" (Acts 12:12). They were united; they were gathered *together*. They were fervently, earnestly praying.

83

They were praying without ceasing. They were praying specifically for Peter. God in His sovereign will had permitted James to be slain, but now they were interceding for Peter. Prayer must always be connected with the sovereignty of God. Prayer is not telling God what to do. Prayer is finding out what God wants to do and asking Him to do it.

Their praying was specific; they prayed for Peter. Their praying was persistent. I get the impression that they had been praying all week and all night. You don't find many all-night prayer meetings today. I recall, in the early days of Youth for Christ, that I used to go to Winona Lake, Indiana, and attend the all-night prayer meetings. Our dear brother, Peter Deyneka, Sr., led those prayer meetings, and what meetings they were!

Here were people who were gathered together to pray in a united, fervent, specific, persistent way, and yet their praying was mingled with doubt! When their prayer was answered, they couldn't believe it! The servant girl Rhoda told them, "Peter is at the door" (see v. 14). They said, "You must be mad!" (see v. 15). They came and discovered that Peter *was* at the door! The weapons of the church's warfare are not physical (see II Cor. 10:3-5). We don't use physical weapons to fight spiritual battles. The church was not arming for battle. The people were not trying to influence the Sanhedrin. They weren't trying to bribe Herod. They weren't holding a demonstration. *They were on their knees praying!* And the hand of God reached down and took care of Herod. At the close of Acts 12, the hand of God moved, and He used some little worms to kill the king who thought he was so great.

The greatest power in the world is the power of prayer that moves the hand of God. Yet it is not easy today to get many people together in somebody's house for prayer. The weapons of our warfare are not carnal; they are spiritual. They are the kind of weapons that tear down strongholds—the way Joshua did when he knocked down the walls of Jericho. God didn't have to blow up the prison to deliver Peter. He simply sent an angel down—not an army but one angel. "The angel fetched Peter out of prison," said Thomas Watson, "but it was prayer that fetched the angel." The angels are our servants. "Are they not all ministering spirits [servants], sent forth to minister [do service] for them who shall be heirs of salvation?" (Heb. 1:14). You and I as God's children have the angelic hosts to help us in our times of need. The trouble is, we don't pray.

I don't know what particular "prison problems" you may have in your church. Perhaps some of your missionaries are going through difficulty. You may have problems with the authorities. You can be sure of this: God answers prayer. No matter what the situation may be, no matter how high the walls, no matter how locked the doors, no matter how strong may be the guards, God is able to deliver. No matter how great the power of Satan may be in the world today, we still have the power of God. People can be delivered and many wonderful things can happen if the church will learn how to pray. "Peter, therefore, was kept in prison; but prayer was made without ceasing by the church unto God for him" (Acts 12:5). Is your church a praying church? Something happens when churches pray, for when churches pray, God's hand begins to work. Doors are opened and deliverance takes place because God's people pray.

Chapter 10

Prayer and Open Doors

In Acts 10 we find two men praying. In the first part of the chapter, verses 1-8, we find Cornelius, a Roman centurion, praying. In verse 9 we find the Apostle Peter praying. As this chapter progresses, Cornelius and Peter get together and prayer is answered. Something happens when churches pray because when people pray, God opens doors of witness and ministry and lost sinners are saved. Consider the account in Acts 10.

"There was a certain man in Caesarea called Cornelius, a centurion of the band called the Italian band, a devout man, and one that feared God with all his house, who gave much alms to the people, and prayed to God always" (vv. 1,2). Cornelius was not a converted man. He was probably a "proselyte of the gate." By that we mean that he was not fully accepted in the Jewish faith. He gave alms, he prayed, he observed the Jewish prayer hours, but he had not been received into Judaism. He knew that his Roman religion was wrong and that all the gods of the Roman religion were false gods. He was seeking the truth. He wanted to know how to be saved. "He saw in a vision evidently [openly] about the ninth hour of the day, an angel of God coming in to him, and saying unto him, Cornelius. And when he looked on him, he was afraid, and said, What is it, Lord? And he said unto him, Thy prayers and thine alms are come up for a memorial before God. And now send men to Joppa, and call for one Simon, whose surname is Peter. He lodgeth with one Simon, a tanner, whose house is by the seaside; he shall tell thee what thou oughtest to do" (vv. 3-6).

At the same time God was speaking to Cornelius, He was also preparing Peter. God always prepares us for what He is preparing for us. The story in Acts 10 continues.

"On the next day, as they [the three men sent from Cornelius] went on their journey, and drew near unto the city, Peter went up upon the housetop to pray about the sixth hour. And he became very hungry, and would have eaten, but while they made ready, he fell into a trance, and saw heaven opened, and a certain vessel descending unto him, as it had been a great sheet knit at the four corners, and let down to the earth; in which were all manner of four-footed beasts of the earth, and wild beasts, and creeping things, and fowls of the air. And there came a voice to him, Rise, Peter; kill, and eat. But Peter said, Not so, Lord; for I have never eaten anything that is common or unclean" (vv. 9-14).

This happened a second and a third time, and Peter was perplexed, wondering what all of this meant. About that time the three visitors arrived at the door, and the Holy Spirit spoke to Peter. "While

Peter thought on the vision, the Spirit said unto him, Behold, three men seek thee. Arise, therefore, and get thee down, and go with them, doubting nothing; for I have sent them" (vv. 19,20). That little phrase "doubting nothing" literally means "making no difference, making no distinction." They were Gentiles, and Peter was a Jew; but he was to go with them because God was about to open up some new doors so that the Gentiles could be saved.

Peter's Prayer

What was Peter praying about when he was on the housetop that noontide? We don't know, but we can try to find out. For one thing, he was hungry. Perhaps his hunger reminded him of something Jesus said in John 4: "My food is to do the will of him that sent me, and to finish his work. Say not ye, There are yet four months, and then cometh harvest? Behold, I say unto you, Lift up your eyes, and look on the fields; for they are white already to harvest" (vv. 34,35). I wonder if, while Peter was hungry, he was thinking about that experience he had with the Lord Jesus when He said, "Peter, open your eyes now and look—there is going to be a harvest." Perhaps he was praying about lost souls. I don't know. The Word of God doesn't tell us. But I wonder if he wasn't praying about the harvest.

Remember, too, it was the sixth hour. At the sixth hour, when Jesus was crucified, darkness covered the earth (see Mark 15:33). I wonder if Peter was thinking about those three hours when the Lord Jesus hung on the cross and was made sin

89

for the whole world. Perhaps Peter was praying, "O Lord, You died for the whole world! You gave Your life for the whole world! Help us to reach out and win more people!"

I notice that Peter was at Joppa. Every Bible student knows that Joppa was the place from which Jonah sailed in his attempt to escape from God. God said, "Jonah, go to the Gentiles." Jonah said, "I'm a Jew. I'm not going to the Gentiles!"

I don't know what Peter was praying about, but I have a suspicion that he was praying about reaching out and winning lost souls to the Lord Jesus Christ.

Cornelius was praying the day before. Here you have a seeking sinner and a praying saint, and God gets the two of them together! I think one reason why we don't see more people come to Christ is because we aren't praying about it. We are supposed to pray that the Word of God will have free course and will touch the lives of people and win them to the Lord Jesus Christ.

Peter was about to open the door of faith to the Gentiles. God gave Peter the keys of the kingdom— not the keys to heaven or the keys to hell but the keys of the kingdom. Peter opened the door of faith to those who needed to believe. In Acts 2 he opened the door of faith to the Jews. In Acts 8 he opened the door of faith to the Samaritans. Here in Acts 10 he was about to open the door of faith to the Gentiles. The key to chapters 10 and 11 is this little phrase, "doubting nothing," which means "making no difference" (10:20). That there is no difference is a basic principle in Scripture, and we want to apply it to several different aspects of our ministry.

No Difference in the Need

To begin with, *there is no difference in the need.* All men are lost. A brand of theology today says that we Christians should not evangelize the lost, that we should not send out missionaries or try to witness. Why? Because everybody has his own religion, and that religion is accepted by God. It's as though all roads lead to Rome or all roads lead to New York, and it makes no difference what road you are on. This kind of theology is not biblical because Jesus said, "I am the way" (John 14:6). Peter said, "There is no other name under heaven given among men, whereby we must be saved" (Acts 4:12). I think it is helpful to have dialogue with people of other faiths. I think it is good to try to understand our neighbors and what they believe. We can better witness to them and minister to them. But we must never dilute the Gospel of Jesus Christ or say that it is just one of many different "Gospels" in the world today. If the Gospel is *the* good news, then any other message of salvation is bad news.

Cornelius was a devout man, a God-fearing man, a giving man, a praying man, apparently a very righteous man and a man of character—and yet he was not saved. If *any* sincere religion will save you, then Cornelius didn't need Peter or Peter's message! But Cornelius knew he needed to be saved. In Acts 11:14, when Peter rehearsed what had hap-

91

pened, he said that the angel told Cornelius, "Who shall tell thee words, by which thou and all thy house shall be saved." Before Peter shared the Gospel with them, these Romans were all lost! There is no difference in the need. All men are lost, and all men need the Gospel.

No Difference in the Method

Second, *there is no difference in the method*. What is God's method for saving people? *The Word of God and prayer*. The whole event seems so complicated! An angel spoke to Cornelius, God sent a vision to Peter three times, and then the Spirit spoke to Peter. The three Gentiles had to travel 30 miles to Joppa to get Peter, and then they had to go 30 miles back to Caesarea. It probably took four days for this trip. According to Acts 8:40, Philip, the evangelist, was already in Caesarea. He could have told Cornelius how to be saved! In fact, the angel could have done it! But God said, "No, My messenger is Peter. I gave Peter the keys. Peter is the one who is going to open the door to the Gentiles." The angel didn't preach the Word of God. If God gave the Gospel to angels and said, "Go convert the world," they would get it done!

No Difference in the Message

Peter was used of God to bring the message to these people because he was a praying Christian, a burdened Christian. He wanted to see the Gospel proclaimed to all. There is no difference in the need—all men are lost. There is no difference in the method—God uses the Gospel, the Word of God, and prayer. *There is no difference in the message.* When you read Peter's message in Acts 10 you discover that he preached that Jesus Christ is the Son of God and that He died for our sins and rose again. Note verse 43: "To him [Jesus] give all the prophets witness, that through his name whosoever believeth in him shall receive remission of sins." That's the Gospel. When those Gentiles heard "whosoever," they believed! "While Peter yet spoke these words, the Holy Spirit fell on all them who heard the word" (v. 44). They believed, and Peter's Jewish friends were amazed that the Gentiles could be saved simply by faith, without first becoming Jews.

No Difference in the Results

There is no difference in the results. When you trust the Lord Jesus Christ as your own Lord and Saviour, the Holy Spirit of God enters your life and you know that you are born again. The same Spirit was given to the Gentiles who had been given to the Jews. Later on, when Peter was asked by the Jews to give an accounting of this event, he told them exactly what happened. "And as I began to speak, the Holy Spirit fell on them, as on us at the beginning" (Acts 11:15). At what beginning? At the beginning of the Church back in Acts 2.

The conversion of Cornelius could well have taken place ten years after Pentecost. We don't have the exact chronology, but it could well have been ten years after Pentecost. God was gradually

93

bringing a transition from Israel to the Church, from the Jews to the Gentiles. He didn't do it suddenly; He did it gradually. It is interesting that Peter had to reach back eight or ten years for an example of the Holy Spirit's baptism. Some say that all through the Book of the Acts the Holy Spirit was baptizing the same people. No, He wasn't. He baptized Peter in Acts 2, and Peter had to reach all the way back to Acts 2 for an example.

The same Spirit was given. The same baptism was administered. Peter said, "These people have received the Holy Spirit. They should be baptized!" He was fulfilling the Great Commission. The same doctrine was taught. Cornelius and his household asked Peter to tarry with them certain days (10:48), and so Peter tarried. Why? So he could teach them the Word of God. This is the way it's supposed to be. First you go out and make disciples, then you baptize them, then you teach them and build them up in Christian fellowship.

The salvation of Cornelius and his household was the result of prayer. I wonder if we don't have unsaved people in our neighborhoods just like Cornelius—moral people, good people, religious people. They probably go to church even more faithfully than some evangelicals do, but they aren't saved. They are nice neighbors, but they aren't saved; and in their hearts they are praying, "O God, send someone to show me how to be saved." If you and I are praying and asking for God's direction, a praying saint and a praying sinner will eventually be brought together by the Holy Spirit of God. I don't think we are asking too much. I think the whole picture in Acts 10 is that of praying for lost souls.

I know some people say we are not supposed to pray for the lost. I don't agree with them. In I Timothy 2:1 Paul said we should pray for *all* men, and that includes the lost. We should pray for lost loved ones, lost neighbors and friends and lost people in other lands. Jesus prayed for the lost (Luke 23:34), and so did Paul (Rom. 10:1).

Peter was on the housetop praying. We aren't told what he was praying about. But I am sure that somewhere in his prayer he said, in effect, "Lord, where do I go next? What do I do now?" He had tarried many days in Joppa according to Acts 9:43. Don't always be on the go; wait for God's leading. Pastor friend, missionary friend, stop long enough for God to say something new to you. Somebody might have said, "What's Peter doing staying with Simon the tanner? Why isn't he busy doing something for the Lord?" He was. He was tarrying, waiting for God to tell him what the next step would be. That's the kind of people God uses—people who pause to pray and to listen. Cornelius was praying, and God honored his request. Peter was praying, and the Holy Spirit began to work in a wonderful way to bring these two together.

There is no difference in the need—all men are lost. There is no difference in the method—God uses people, praying people, to get the Gospel out. There is no difference in the message. The same message that converted Peter also converted Cornelius. There is no difference in the results: The

95

same Holy Spirit is given, and the same baptism is administered. Please note that these people were saved *before they were baptized*. This answers those who argue, "You must be baptized to be saved." I believe that saved people ought to be baptized. I do not believe that baptism is a part of salvation. These people were already saved, possessing the Holy Spirit and magnifying God, before they were baptized.

Something happens when churches pray, for then God opens the doors of faith to lost sinners and then the Gospel reaches out to change their lives.

Chapter 11

Prayer and the "Key" Christian

The history of the Church is the record of the conflict between closed minds and open doors. As you read the history of the Church, beginning in the Book of the Acts, you find that wherever God had praying people, there were open doors. Wherever God had people like the Apostle Peter in Acts 10 and 11, there were open doors of ministry. Exciting new things were happening because people were praying. But whenever you find people who are praying, people who are excited about open doors, you also find people with closed minds, people who look at the future in a rearview mirror. You meet head-on the conflict with people who cannot change and who will not change.

We read in Acts 10 that Peter was praying and that God gave him a vision. God told him that the Gentiles would be reached with the Gospel. At first Peter had a closed mind himself. In Acts 10:14 Peter said, "Not so, Lord; for I have never eaten anything that is common or unclean." God taught Peter that the Gentiles were now to be a part of the Church. Peter was going to use his keys for the third time. He had opened the door of faith to the Jews at

97

Pentecost (ch. 2), and he had opened the door of faith for the Samaritans (ch. 8). In Acts 10 Peter opened the door of faith for the Gentiles. God moved him into an exciting new area of ministry.

Peter was a "key" Christian, and yet he was criticized for what he did. I've noticed as I have read church history and Christian biographies that whenever God calls someone to do something new, that person is opposed, even by Christian people. There are always those who are "sanctified obstructionists," who stand in the way of progress. They are sincere, but they are blind and shackled to the past. They are sincere, but they are so bound by tradition that they cannot change. This is a tragedy because, though the Gospel does not change and the message of the Word of God does not change, God's Church must adapt itself to the new things that He is doing.

The Apostle Peter was God's "key" man. He was opening the doors of faith. In Acts 11 Peter ran in to some closed minds, and he had to defend himself. "The apostles and brethren that were in Judaea heard that the Gentiles had also received the word of God. And when Peter was come up to Jerusalem, they that were of the circumcision [the legalistic party in the church] contended with him" (vv. 1,2). The phrase "contended with him" means they made a difference with him. It's the same phrase that's used in Acts 10:20 where the Spirit of God said to Peter, "Arise, therefore, and get thee down, and go with them, doubting nothing." The phrase "doubting nothing" means "making no difference,

98

making no distinction." We discovered in our previous study that there is no difference between Gentiles and Jews. Both are lost, and both need to be saved by faith.

The legalists in the church had closed minds, and they contended with Peter. They made a difference. They wanted to make a distinction between Jewish believers and Gentile believers. They said, "Thou wentest in to men uncircumcised, and didst eat with them. But Peter reviewed the matter from the beginning, and expounded it in order unto them, saying, I was in the city of Joppa praying; and in a trance I saw a vision, a certain vessel descending, as it had been a great sheet, let down from heaven by four corners, and it came even to me; upon which, when I had fastened mine eyes, I considered, and saw four-footed beasts of the earth, and wild beasts, and creeping things, and fowls of the air. And I heard a voice saying unto me, Arise, Peter; slay and eat. But I said, Not so, Lord; for nothing common or unclean hath at any time entered into my mouth. But the voice answered me again from heaven, What God hath cleansed, that call not thou common. And this was done three times; and all were drawn up again into heaven. And, behold, immediately there were three men already come unto the house where I was, sent from Caesarea unto me. And the Spirit bade me go with them, nothing doubting [making no difference]. Moreover, these six brethren accompanied me, and we entered into the man's house" (11:3-12).

Then Peter went on to tell how he preached the

99

Word of God: "And as I began to speak, the Holy Spirit fell on them, as on us at the beginning. Then remembered I the word of the Lord, how he said, John indeed baptized with water; but ye shall be baptized with the Holy Spirit. Forasmuch, then, as God gave them the same gift as he did unto us, who believed on the Lord Jesus Christ, what was I, that I could withstand God?" (vv. 15-17).

Peter was a key man. God was using him to open doors. What are the marks of a key Christian? Do you and I have open doors or closed minds? I've discovered in my ministry that when people are praying and seeking the will of God, God opens doors for them. They have places of ministry, and God gives them exciting opportunities for witness. What are the marks of a key Christian? There are at least four of them, and Peter illustrated these four marks of a key Christian.

His Eyes

First, you can always tell a key Christian by his eyes: *He sees the vision.* You and I are not about to see the same vision that Peter saw. God is not going to send down a sheet, filled with all kinds of animals, for us to look at. But God does want us to see the need. "But when he [Jesus] saw the multitudes, he was moved with compassion on them, because they were faint, and were scattered abroad, as sheep having no shepherd. Then saith he unto his disciples, The harvest truly is plenteous, but the laborers are few. Pray ye, therefore, the Lord of the harvest, that he will send forth laborers into his harvest"

(Matt. 9:36-38). The Lord wants us to see this lost world as a flock that needs shepherding and as a field that needs harvesting. Do you see that? Are you the kind of Christian who, because you pray, has seen the vision of a lost world?

Why don't some Christians see this vision? Why do some Christians have closed minds and closed eyes? Some people don't see because they are spiritually dead. Jesus said, "Except a man be born again, he cannot see the kingdom of God" (John 3:3). Until your eyes are opened by faith, until you trust Jesus as Saviour, you cannot see what this world is really like.

Some Christians are blind to the vision because of spiritual deficiency. They are spiritually alive, but they are not spiritually healthy. Doctors tell us that diet affects vision. This is especially true of people who may have some chemical problems in their body. Diet affects vision. In II Peter 1:5-7 Peter wrote about Christian growth: "Giving all diligence, add to your faith virtue; and to virtue, knowledge; and to knowledge, self-control; and to self-control, patience; and to patience, godliness; and to godliness, brotherly kindness; and to brotherly kindness, love." Verses 8 and 9 say, "For if these things be in you, and abound, they make you that ye shall neither be barren nor unfruitful in the knowledge of our Lord Jesus Christ. But he that lacketh these things is blind and cannot see afar off, and hath forgotten that he was purged from his old sins." Some Christians, because they are not growing, cannot see the vision.

Some cannot see because they are distracted. They put their hand to the plow, and they looked back (see Luke 9:62). Or like Lot, they are looking around at the world and have taken their eyes off the field.

Do you see this world today as a flock that needs shepherding, as a field that needs harvesting? Do you see the vision? Are you the kind of praying Christian who, when you look upon this world, sees that God wants you to do something? You can always tell a key Christian by his or her eyes. A key Christian sees the vision. There is a job to be done. There are people to be reached with the Gospel.

His Ears

You can tell the key Christian not only by his eyes but also by his ears: *He hears the voice.* Peter said, "I heard a voice saying unto me, 'Arise, Peter, slay and eat' " (see Acts 10:13). Have you heard the voice of God commanding you to go?

Some years ago, a very good friend of mine, Dr. E. Myers Harrison, gave a missionary message that I cannot forget. It was to a small group of people, but I will never forget the sermon. Dr. Harrison is now at home with the Lord, but he was a great servant of God and a great missionary statesman. He said that each of us as Christians must hear what God has to say. There is *the command from above:* "Go ye into all the world, and preach the gospel to every creature" (Mark 16:15). Have you heard that? I've heard people say, "But God wants our church to be different. We're not supposed to have a missionary program." I don't believe that. I believe the command from above is given to every Christian and to every assembly that God has raised up.

Then there is *the cry from beneath*. Remember the rich man who died and woke up in hell and begged for someone to go and tell his brothers? (see Luke 16). "I pray thee, therefore, father, that thou wouldest send him to my father's house (for I have five brethren), that he may testify unto them, lest they also come into this place of torment" (vv. 27,28). There is the cry from beneath. If you and I could hear the cries of people in a lost eternity right now, we'd realize how important it is to get the Gospel out. There's the command from above. Have you heard it? There's the cry from beneath. Have you heard it?

Then, according to Dr. Harrison, there is *the call from without*. Acts 16:9 says, "Come over into Macedonia, and help us." People around us are saying, "Please come to help us!" So much money, time and energy is being spent on routine church matters in America when there is a whole world to reach for Christ! We face so many open doors! This world is a flock that needs shepherding and a field that needs harvesting. People are crying out, "Come over and help us!"

His Feet

You can always tell a key Christian by his eyes— he sees the vision—and by his ears—he hears the voice. "Today if ye will hear his voice, harden not your hearts" (Heb. 3:15). Third, you can always tell a key Christian by his feet: *He makes the venture*. Peter got up and went. The Spirit told him to go, nothing doubting. So he went. This was an act of faith. Peter knew that he was going to the Gentiles and that the Jews were not to mix with the Gentiles. There was a wall between them. And yet Peter dared to be a pioneer. He dared to have an open mind as he faced these open doors, because Peter was a man of prayer.

At one time Peter had *wayward* feet, but Andrew brought him to Jesus. And then one night Peter had some *wet* feet because he was walking on the water. Then he had *washed* feet when Jesus knelt before him and washed his feet (John 13). He had *wandering* feet when he denied the Lord. Here he had *willing* feet. "How beautiful are the feet of them that preach the gospel of peace" (Rom. 10:15). What kind of feet do you have?

His Lips

You can always tell a key Christian by his eyes (he sees the vision), by his ears (he hears the voice) and by his feet (he makes the venture). He doesn't just pray about it—he does something. Finally, you can always tell a key Christian by his lips: *He shares the victory*.

The Apostle Peter came to the household of Cornelius and shared the Word of God—that Jesus Christ died and was raised from the dead and that anybody can be saved by faith. "That through his name whosoever believeth in him shall receive remission of sins" (Acts 10:43). Some wanted to close this door. The Holy Spirit had opened the door, but some wanted to close it. The legalists wanted to close the door (see ch. 11). They said, "Peter, you were wrong. You should never have done that. A Gentile must become a Jew before he can become a Christian" (see vv. 1-3). Peter said, "No, the Holy Spirit said it's not that way at all. We are not going to make any difference. Who was I that I could withstand God?" (see vv. 12-18).

In Acts 15 this same legalistic crowd tried to close the door again. A great contention, a real argument, occurred between Paul, Peter, Barnabas and the church. Thank God they came to the conclusion that Gentiles do not have to become Jews to become Christians. It's interesting to note that throughout the Book of the Acts somebody is usually trying to close the door. The history of the Church is really the record of conflict between closed minds and open doors. You can always tell the key Christian by his lips. He shares the victory. He tells others what God is doing.

Are you one of God's "key" Christians? Are you a door opener? Is your church moving forward in pioneer advance into new fields of ministry because you have the eyes to see the vision, the ears to hear the voice, the feet to make the venture and the lips to share the victory? Are you opening doors or closing doors? Are you a key Christian?

Something happens when churches pray because, when churches pray, God opens doors. Sometimes God has to open closed minds, closed eyes, closed

105

ears and closed hearts. Something happens when churches pray, because the Spirit of God does a wonderful work as key Christians walk through open doors to do exciting things to the glory of God.

Chapter 12

Prayer and a Lost World

If you and I had visited the city of Antioch in Syria about the year A.D. 45, we would have seen a beautiful metropolis. Antioch was called "Antioch the beautiful, Queen of the East." About half a million people lived in Antioch. It was a cosmopolitan city, a great center of trade and business. The imperial mint was there and also the center for government. But the most important people in Antioch were not at the Board of Trade or the mint or the capitol building. The most important people in Antioch were meeting together, worshiping God and praying.

"Now there were in the church that was at Antioch certain prophets and teachers, as Barnabas, and Symeon, who was called Niger, and Lucius of Cyrene, and Manaen, who had been brought up with Herod, the tetrarch, and Saul. As they ministered to the Lord, and fasted, the Holy Spirit said, Separate me Barnabas and Saul for the work unto which I have called them. And when they had fasted and prayed, and laid their hands on them, they sent them away. So they, being sent forth by the Holy

Spirit, departed unto Seleucia; and from there they sailed to Cyprus" (Acts 13:1-4).

This was the beginning of the worldwide missionary outreach of the Church. In Acts 2 Peter had opened the door of faith to the Jews, in Acts 8 to the Samaritans and in Acts 10 to the Gentiles. But all of this ministry had been very close to home. The pattern given in Acts 1:8 required the Church to begin in Jerusalem, then go to all Judea and Samaria and then to the uttermost parts of the earth. The Apostle Paul was going to be the key man to take the Gospel to the Gentiles, who needed the Lord Jesus Christ so desperately.

The most important people in Antioch were the people who were meeting together in that church assembly, worshiping God and praying. This was the beginning of the worldwide missionary outreach of the Church.

This raises a very important question: What is the relationship between prayer and reaching a lost world with the Gospel? I don't think anybody has to be convinced that it is the task of the local church to reach the lost world with the Gospel. We must witness not only in our own Jerusalem (where we are living) and to neighboring areas, but we also need to reach out to the uttermost parts of the earth.

It's a sad thing when a local church becomes ingrown, when the Gospel becomes a commodity to protect instead of a treasure to share. It's a sad thing when the pastor does not proclaim the needs of a lost world, not just the needs of a lost city or a lost neighborhood. I agree with Dr. Oswald J. Smith that the light that shines the farthest is going to shine the brightest at home. I don't think the church should ignore missions just to promote local evangelism. Both are important.

The church in Antioch was meeting together, and the leaders were ministering. The word "ministering" means "serving the Lord in a priestly fashion." The Greek word gives us our English word "liturgy." As they ministered to the Lord, praying and worshiping, the Holy Spirit of God began to work. From that church the first missionaries to the Gentiles went out.

What is the relationship between prayer and reaching a lost world with the Gospel? I think the answer is this: Prayer meets a twofold need in the ministry of missionary outreach. First, prayer supplies the workers, and second, prayer supports the workers.

Prayer Supplies the Workers

Our Lord Jesus made a statement in Luke 10 that every Christian must heed. "After these things the Lord appointed other seventy also, and sent them two by two before his face into every city and place, where he himself would come. Therefore said he unto them, The harvest truly is great, but the laborers are few; pray ye, therefore the Lord of the harvest, that he would send forth laborers into his harvest" (vv. 1,2).

The harvest truly is great. We have no problem believing that. You can look at your neighborhood and know that the harvest is great. I trust that you read the missionary news in various magazines, perhaps your own denominational publications, perhaps our *Good News Broadcaster*. This will help you realize the tremendous harvest that is just waiting for laborers. The problem is not lack of a harvest, the problem is that we don't have enough laborers.

If you want to know *why* we don't have the laborers, look at Luke 9:57-62. "It came to pass that, as they went on the way, a certain man said unto him, Lord, I will follow thee wherever thou goest" (v. 57). Ah, here's a volunteer! "Jesus said unto him, Foxes have holes, and birds of the air have nests, but the Son of man hath not where to lay his head" (v. 58). And that's the last we hear of this fellow. Why? He was looking for comfort and security, and he couldn't find them.

Jesus said to another, "Follow me" (v. 59). Here's one who was called. The Son spoke and said, "Follow Me." What a privilege! What a challenge! But he said, "Lord, permit me first to go and bury my father. Jesus said unto him, Let the dead bury their dead; but go thou and preach the kingdom of God" (vv. 59,60). There's nothing wrong with taking care of your family, nothing wrong with showing respect for your father. But notice his statement, "Permit me first." That's bad grammar, but it's also bad theology. We should not put ourselves first; we should put the Lord first. "Another also said, Lord, I will follow thee; but let me first go bid them farewell, who are at home at my house. And Jesus said unto

110

him, No man, having put his hand to the plough, and looking back, is fit for the kingdom of God" (vv. 61,62).

This is why the laborers are few. People like to sing, "I'll go where You want me to go," but they won't go. They pray, "O God, supply workers." But they won't be available themselves. Prayer supplies the workers. We are commanded to pray that the Lord of the Harvest will send out laborers into the harvest field. Are you doing that? Pastor, when you pray on Sundays, do you pray, "O God, Lord of the Harvest, call laborers from our church to go out and do the job"?

Notice in Acts 13 that God went to the beginning of the list and called Barnabas and then to the end of the list and called Saul, and He put those two together. Later on it became Saul and Barnabas and then Paul and Barnabas as Paul became the leader of the ministry. Barnabas and Saul were two of that church's best men.

What would happen to your church if God called your pastor to go to the mission field? You say, "We would lose our pastor." You'd *send* your pastor— you wouldn't lose him. You'd *keep* him because he would be going out and building up the Church around the world. We get selfish in local churches. We do not pray that the Lord of the Harvest will send forth laborers. Are you willing to give your best young people? Are you willing to give your best young couples? God may want to speak to a businessman in your church. Are you willing to let him go, or are you thinking only of building up your own

111

local church here at home? The church that does not pray for laborers is disobeying the Word of God.

It's interesting to note that this group was not meeting in a missionary conference. They were serving the Lord in their regular ministry. They were preaching and teaching, serving God and winning souls. They were worshiping and praying. While they were involved in a worship service, God called two of their best men to go to the mission field.

This is what happened to Isaiah. He went into the temple to pray. The throne on earth was empty, but the throne in heaven was full. He saw the glory of God, and he heard a voice that said, "Whom shall I send, and who will go for us?" (Isa. 6:8). Isaiah said, "Here am I; send me" (v. 8). He went into the service as a worshiper, and he walked out as a worker. He went into the service as a spectator and came out as a participant. His life was turned around.

Prayer supplies workers. The Holy Spirit asked for their two best men, and the church willingly released them. "As they ministered to the Lord, and fasted, the Holy Spirit said, Separate me Barnabas and Saul for the work unto which I have called them. And when they had fasted and prayed, and laid their hands on them, they sent them away" (Acts 13:2,3). The Greek says, "They turned them loose, they freed them." They said, "You are free from the work here. Go out and do what God wants you to do." The whole church was involved in praying. Prayer supplies workers. That's the first need that is met when we pray.

Prayer Supports the Workers

Second, prayer supports the workers. How do you pray for missionaries? When Barnabas and Paul left the church of Antioch, how did these people pray for them? I suggest you read Paul's letters and find out what his prayer requests were. So often we hear people praying, "Lord, bless the missionaries." But what does that mean? As we pray about various needs, it would be wise for us to listen to Paul's prayer requests. How do you pray for the people who are serving the Lord on the mission field?

Romans 15:30 says, "Now I beseech you, brethren, for the Lord Jesus Christ's sake, and for the love of the Spirit, that ye strive together with me in your prayers to God for me." The word "strive" means "to agonize." "That I may be delivered from them that do not believe in Judaea" (v. 31). There's the first request—for personal safety, for protection. Do you pray for the protection of your missionaries? There are enemies on the mission field who hate the Gospel, who hate missionaries. "And that my service, which I have for Jerusalem, may be accepted by the saints" (v. 31). Here he was asking for God's blessing on his ministry. He was taking a special missionary offering to the saints in Jerusalem.

Here are two requests—deliverance from the

Enemy and blessing on the ministry. "That I may come unto you with joy by the will of God" (v. 32). He was requesting God's guidance in his travels and God's direction in his plans. Do you pray that God will direct the missionaries as they travel, as they use their time? "And may with you be refreshed" (v. 32). Do you pray for spiritual and physical refreshment for the missionaries?

Here are four very special requests—for personal deliverance, for blessing on the ministry, for guidance and wisdom in travel and making plans, and for spiritual and physical refreshment. Second Corinthians 1:9-11 says, "But we had the sentence of death in ourselves, that we should not trust in ourselves but in God, who raiseth the dead, who delivered us from so great a death, and doth deliver; in whom we trust that he will yet deliver us, ye also helping together by prayer for us." He was saying, "I went through great difficulty. Please pray that God will give us the deliverance that we need." We never know what our missionaries are going through. We must pray for their physical and spiritual protection.

He prayed the same thing in Philippians 1. He was in prison, about to be tried for his faith. Verse 19 says, "For I know that this shall turn to my salvation through your prayer, and the supply of the Spirit of Jesus Christ." In II Thessalonians 3:1 Paul prayed, "Finally, brethren, pray for us, that the word of the Lord may have free course, and be glorified, even as it is with you."

Do you pray that God will bless the teaching and preaching of His Word? Pray for literature, cassette, radio and television ministries. Are you praying that God will give His Word great success and that His servants will be delivered from unreasonable and wicked men? Satan would like to destroy all of God's servants!

Ephesians 6:18,19 says, "Praying always with all prayer and supplication in the Spirit, and watching thereunto with all perseverance and supplication for all saints; and for me, that utterance may be given unto me." Do you ever pray about language study or about preaching in a foreign language? "That utterance may be given unto me, that I may open my mouth boldly to make known the mystery of the gospel, for which I am an ambassador in bonds" (vv. 19,20). Paul didn't say, "Pray that my prison doors might be opened." He wrote: "Pray that my mouth might be opened so that I can share the Word of God as I should." He said it also in Colossians 4:3,4: "Praying also for us, that God would open unto us a door of utterance, to speak the mystery of Christ, for which I am also in bonds; that I may make it manifest, as I ought to speak."

These are some of the prayer requests that Paul shared with his praying congregations. I'm sure the people at Antioch probably prayed this way when they sent Barnabas and Saul on their way: "Father, protect them as they travel. Give them wisdom as they travel. Guide them so that they might make the right decisions in the use of their time. Protect them from the Evil One. Protect them from wicked people who don't agree with the Gospel. Bless what they say. Bless as they preach the Word of God.

115

Help them as they share the Word of God with people who have never heard it before!"

In Romans 1:10 Paul said this: "Making request, if by any means now at length I might have a prosperous journey by the will of God to come unto you." We should pray that God will give spiritual and physical prosperity to His missionaries. Oh, that we would pray earnestly, agonizing in prayer, that God might use His servants for His glory!

Something happens when churches pray, because as churches pray, God can call out people to serve Him in other places. The harvest is great. The laborers are few. Are you praying that God will supply the workers? Something happens when churches pray, because when churches pray, God supports the workers and gives them all they need to accomplish the work He wants them to accomplish. One of our great needs today is for God's people to be praying for our missionary laborers— praying that God will use them and bless them so that they might win many souls to Christ.

Chapter 13

The Model Prayer—Relationship

In many churches the Lord's Prayer is used frequently, if not regularly, in the services. This prayer is recorded in Matthew 6 as well as in Luke 11. Here is Matthew's account:

"After this manner, therefore, pray ye: Our Father, who art in heaven, Hallowed be thy name. Thy kingdom come. Thy will be done in earth, as it is in heaven. Give us this day our daily bread. And forgive us our debts, as we forgive our debtors. And lead us not into temptation, but deliver us from evil. For thine is the kingdom, and the power, and the glory, forever. Amen" (vv. 9-13).

This prayer was given to be a model for our own praying. Our Lord did not say, "In these words, pray." Rather, He said, "After this manner, therefore, pray" (v. 9). I see nothing wrong with Christians' praying this prayer from their hearts. To be sure, reciting this prayer can become a ritual; but then many times our own praying becomes a ritual! The fault does not lie with the prayer; the fault lies with the one who is doing the praying. I have been in some services where this prayer was merely recited

117

from the lips. I have also been in services where the congregation prayed this prayer from their hearts, and it was a very moving experience. I am not saying that we *must* use this prayer in our public meetings. The early church did use this prayer. I am saying that the Lord's Prayer is a model for us to follow in our own praying. If churches and individuals are to pray effectively, they need to model their praying after this particular prayer.

In the Lord's Prayer (or the Disciples' Prayer) we have three essentials for effective praying. First, there is *relationship:* "Our Father, who art in heaven" (v. 9). Then there is *responsibility:* "Hallowed be thy name. Thy kingdom come. Thy will be done" (vv. 9,10). Finally, there are *requests:* "Give us this day our daily bread. And forgive us our debts, as we forgive our debtors. And lead us not into temptation, but deliver us from evil" (vv. 11-13). These are the three essentials for effective praying. If we will include these essentials in our praying, God can begin to work in a very wonderful way.

First, there must be a right relationship to others, "*Our* Father," and then to the Lord, "Our *Father*." There must also be responsibility. In our praying we must be concerned about honoring the Father's name, hastening the coming of His kingdom and accomplishing His will on the earth. You will notice that in this prayer, before we ever talk to God about our own personal needs, we should be concerned about *Him:* the glory of His name, the coming of His kingdom and the accomplishing of His will on earth.

Relationship, responsibility and, finally, requests.

If our relationship to others and to the Lord is what it ought to be and if our responsibility is being fulfilled—we want God's name glorified, God's kingdom established and God's will done—then we can come with our requests. In much of our praying, we begin with our requests. We say, "*My* Father," not "*Our* Father." We immediately ask Him for things! We are like the Prodigal Son: "Father, give me!" We beg for things without ever stopping to think about God's name, God's kingdom or God's will. Relationship, responsibility, requests—these are the three essentials for effective praying.

Relationship to God's Family

Let's consider the first essential, relationship. "Our Father, who art in heaven" (Matt. 6:9). This is a twofold relationship—a relationship to God's family, "*Our* Father," and a relationship to God Himself, "Our *Father*." It's rather interesting that there are no *singular* pronouns in the Lord's Prayer. If you or I were going to write this prayer, it would not begin, "Our Father" but "My Father." It would not say, "Give us this day" but "Give *me* this day *my* daily bread."

Throughout this prayer, the Lord Jesus Christ pointed out that we are part of a family. You may pray in solitude, but you can never pray alone. You may pray in solitude, in your own room, but you can never pray independently. The spirit of independence that creeps into our prayer life is what weak-

119

ens our prayer life. No Christian can ever pray alone. He is a part of a great family, the family of God.

The Apostle Paul pointed this out in Ephesians 3:14,15: "For this cause I bow my knees unto the Father of our Lord Jesus Christ, of whom the whole family in heaven and earth is named." Not just my denomination or my church or my family or myself— the "whole family in heaven and earth." In Ephesians 4:17,18 he wrote: "That ye . . . may be able to comprehend, with all saints"—not just some of the saints! He was talking about *all* of the family of God. It's too bad when our praying gets selfish. It's too bad when all we think about is *our* church, *our* Sunday School class, what *we* want. In our praying, we have no right to ask God for anything that is going to help us but hurt another person. If I love you, I won't ask for something that will hurt you. In our praying, we must be very careful to pray, "*Our* Father."

How can I maintain a good relationship with God's family? If I am not in a good relationship with you, I cannot pray to my Father. We have the idea in evangelical churches today that we can fight with each other and then come to the Father and pray. The Word of God says no. If I don't love my brother, if I'm not concerned about my brother, if our church is not concerned about the church up the street where they are preaching the Gospel, then our prayer life is going to be hindered.

To begin with, I must have *a forgiving spirit toward my brother*. If I come to pray and have an

120

unforgiving spirit in my heart, God will not answer. Our Lord said in Matthew 6:14,15, "For if ye forgive men their trespasses, your heavenly Father will also forgive you; but if ye forgive not men their trespasses, neither will your Father forgive your trespasses." We don't *earn* forgiveness, but we show by a forgiving spirit that our heart is prepared to receive God's forgiveness. If I don't forgive you, why should God forgive me? It's not a matter of Law, it's a matter of understanding the grace of God. I must have a forgiving spirit. "When ye stand praying, forgive," said the Lord Jesus (Mark 11:25). When you and I pray, we cannot say, "Our Father" if there is something between us and another brother.

Second, our relationship to other believers involves *humility*. Sometimes our praying turns out to be boasting. The Lord Jesus Christ told a parable about two men who went to the temple to pray. "And he spoke this parable unto certain who trusted in themselves that they were righteous, and despised others: two men went up into the temple to pray; the one a Pharisee, and the other a tax collector. The Pharisee stood and prayed thus with himself, God, I thank thee that I am not as other men are, extortioners, unjust, adulterers, or even as this tax collector" (Luke 18:9-11). This man could not say, "Our Father." Why? Because he was not in good relationship with his brother. Humility is important. We must not come to the throne of grace bragging about ourselves and telling God how much better we are than others, how much more

121

faithful we are, how many more souls we win to Christ. That will only hinder our prayer life.

There must be *unity among God's people*. In I Timothy 2:8 the Apostle Paul wrote: "I will, therefore, that men pray everywhere, lifting up holy hands, without wrath and doubting." When the Jews prayed, they lifted up their hands in prayer. They expected to get something! But we must not show off in our praying as the Pharisees did. "Without wrath and doubting" means "without anger and disputing." Here's a board meeting where men have been fussing with each other, maybe even arguing with each other. Some board members have ill feelings, and then someone says, "Well, let's pray." Those ill feelings have to be taken care of before anybody is ready to pray!

If we are to be in a right relationship with others, we must have a forgiving spirit, humility, unity and *unselfishness*. In James 4:1-3 James talked about selfishness in praying. "Ye ask, and receive not, because ye ask amiss, that ye may consume it upon your lusts" (v. 3). This was causing wars and fighting among the saints to whom James was writing. Selfishness in our praying is destructive. It's terrible the way some people pray as though they are the only ones God ever listens to.

Finally, we must have *love*. If we are not loving one another, God will not hear or answer our prayers. This is especially true of husbands and wives. Peter told Christian wives how they should dress and act so as to help their husbands (see I Pet. 3). Then he told the husbands, "In like manner, ye

122

husbands, dwell with them according to knowledge, giving honor unto the wife, as unto the weaker vessel, and as being heirs together of the grace of life, that your prayers be not hindered" (v. 7). If a husband is not treating his wife the way he should, his prayers are going to be hindered.

We must have a good relationship with one another—in the home, in the church, in the community. We must have a forgiving spirit, humility, unity, unselfishness and love if we want to pray, "Our Father."

Relationship to God Himself

This opening phrase also demands a right relationship to God—"Our *Father*." True prayer is talking to the Father. In one sense God is the Father of everyone since He is the Creator. But we are talking here about being related to the Father *spiritually*. He is the Father only to those who have trusted His Son as their Saviour. We pray to the Father through the Son in the Holy Spirit. To be able to say, "Our Father," you have to be in the family of God.

God is gracious and kind. God can answer the prayers of unbelieving people, but He doesn't have to. God causes the sun to rise on the evil and the good. He sends the rain on the just and on the unjust. He is a gracious and merciful God. He heard the prayers of Cornelius (Acts 10), and He can hear the prayers of unsaved people if He wants to. But no unsaved person can say, "Our Father" because he doesn't belong to the family of God. It is so impor-

123

tant that we have a good relationship with God, and this begins with salvation.

It also involves faith. We must trust God. Mark 11:24 says, "Therefore, I say unto you, Whatever things ye desire, when ye pray, believe that ye receive them, and ye shall have them." Our Lord was saying, "Trust your Father." We trust *earthly* fathers to meet our needs; certainly we ought to be able to trust our Heavenly Father.

If I am to have a good relationship to the Father in heaven, I must be born again, I must have faith in Him, and I must be in the Word of God.

John 15:7 says, "If ye abide in me, and my words abide in you, ye shall ask what ye will, and it shall be done unto you." I must know His Word. In prayer I talk to the Father; when I read the Word, the Father talks to me. Prayer is not a one-way street. Prayer is not a monologue—it's a dialogue. I must listen to what the Father says in the Word if I expect Him to listen to what I have to say at the throne of grace.

I must also have a clean heart. "If I regard iniquity in my heart, the Lord will not hear me" (Ps. 66:18). That word "regard" means "to know that something evil is there, to approve of it and to keep it there." To "regard iniquity" means I see something in my life that is wrong but refuse to deal with it. If I have that kind of heart condition, I cannot really say, "Father" because I am out of fellowship with God.

"Our Father, who art in heaven" (Matt. 6:9). True praying begins with a right relationship to other Christians and a right relationship to the Father in heaven. This means a clean heart, a heart that listens to the Word, a believing heart, a heart that is truly born again through faith in Jesus Christ. Yes, something happens when Christians pray, "Our Father, who art in heaven." It brings unity to God's people, for we cannot pray aright if we are out of fellowship with one another. And it brings fellowship with the Father. It brings joy to the Father's heart, and it brings glory to the Father's name.

Chapter 14

The Model Prayer—Responsibility

The Lord's Prayer, as recorded in Matthew 6, presents to us the essentials for effective praying: relationship, responsibility and request. When God's children pray, they must have a right relationship with each other and with their Father in heaven. This means trusting God. This means knowing Him personally as your Father. This means having the assurance that you are a child of God and that you are obeying Him. Effective praying begins with relationship.

Honor God's Name

But effective praying also involves *responsibility*. Here we see the first three requests in the Lord's Prayer: "Hallowed be thy name. Thy kingdom come. Thy will be done in earth, as it is in heaven" (Matt. 6:9,10). We have a threefold responsibility if we are going to pray effectively: We must honor God's name, hasten God's kingdom and obey God's will.

"Hallowed be thy name" (v. 9). The name of God represents the total of all that He is. A person's name really represents that person, and God is concerned about the glory of His name. We read in Ecclesiastes 7:1: "A good name is better than precious ointment." Proverbs 22:1 says, "A good name is rather to be chosen than great riches." Each of us wants to have a good name. When we sign a check, we want the banker to say, "Yes, I know him. He has a good name." Sometimes you hear about people who left a bad name behind.

God is concerned about His name; He wants His name to be glorified. This is what the Lord Jesus Christ did when He was here on earth. "Father, glorify thy name" (John 12:28). In His prayer, recorded in John 17, our Lord said, "I have glorified thee on the earth; I have finished the work which thou gavest me to do" (v. 4).

The purpose of prayer is to glorify God's name. It is not to glorify our own name. I'm convinced that many of the blessings we see in our ministries come because people we don't even know are praying. I've pastored three different churches, and I know that the blessings God gave us were not primarily because I was the pastor! It was because people were praying. Charles Spurgeon said, when he was asked the secret of his ministry, "My people pray for me." Many anonymous people in our churches today, people we don't think are very important, really *are* important because they pray.

The purpose of prayer is to honor God's name. Everything God does, He does for the glory of His name. If *I* did that, it would be pride. For me to magnify my own name would be arrogant. But the

127

greatest thing in the world is for God to magnify His name, because He is the greatest of all beings in the world. Nothing is higher than the glory of God's name.

When you read the Book of the Acts, you discover many references to the name of Jesus. In the name of Jesus, Peter and John healed the lame man (see ch. 3). When the apostles were arrested, they were told no longer to preach in that name. Peter said, "There is no other name under heaven given among men, whereby we must be saved" (4:12). When the church prayed, they prayed that God's name might be glorified and magnified (v. 30). Everything done in the Book of the Acts was identified with the name of the Lord Jesus Christ.

When I pray, even before I mention daily bread, forgiveness or guidance, I must ask myself, *If God grants these requests, will it honor His name? Am I praying selfishly that I might be honored, or am I praying and trusting Him to answer so that He might be honored?* God in His grace has given us the use of His name. That's a remarkable thing. If some drunken, bankrupt bum stopped you on the street and handed you a note from the bank and said, "Would you sign this for me?" you would be shocked. You wouldn't sign your name to the note of somebody like that. And yet God has given His name to us! We wear His name. We are Christians. We belong to the Church that is identified by His name, "the church of the living God" (I Tim. 3:15). We use His name in prayer. We use His name in worship and in praise. God in His grace has entrusted His name to us. What are we doing with that name?

I sometimes think that some of our prayer requests would never get beyond this first responsibility—honoring God's name. If you're praying about something and God is not answering, ask yourself the question, *If God did answer, would it honor His name?*

Hasten God's Kingdom

The second responsibility we have is to hasten the coming of God's kingdom. "Thy kingdom come" (Matt. 6:10). The Greek verb in that phrase means "to come as a crisis, to come instantly." The Lord was not talking about a process. The *spiritual* kingdom is with us right now. When a person is born again, he enters into the kingdom of God. The Lord Jesus Christ is in heaven as a king and a priest. According to the Book of Hebrews, He is a priest after the order of Melchizedek, and Melchizedek was a king and a priest. I sometimes hear people say, "When Jesus Christ was here on earth, He was the prophet. Now He's in heaven serving as the priest. One day He shall come as the king." But He's enthroned as king right now! Today He is our Melchizedek, seated on the throne. He is the king of righteousness and the king of peace. Righteousness and peace come only through Jesus Christ.

The kingdom of God is here spiritually. Wherever Jesus is, the kingdom is there. But the Bible teaches us that one day He will return and establish a glorious kingdom on the earth. We read in Revelation

11:15: "And the seventh angel sounded; and there were great voices in heaven, saying, The kingdom of this world is become the kingdom of our Lord, and of his Christ, and he shall reign forever and ever." So our Lord Jesus Christ one day shall return and establish His kingdom.

The kingdom of God today is in the hearts of people. We don't see God's kingdom on this earth as it will be when He returns, when the lion and the lamb lie down together, when there will be peace and when men will beat their swords into plowshares. Can believers have any part in hastening the coming of this kingdom?

An interesting reference is found in II Peter 3. Peter wrote about the fact that one day the elements will melt with a fervent heat and the Day of the Lord will come. The earth and the works in it will be burned up. In II Peter 3:11,12 he made this application: "Seeing, then, that all these things shall be dissolved, what manner of persons ought ye to be in all holy living and godliness, looking for and hasting unto the coming of the day of God." That little phrase "hasting unto" can be translated "hastening the coming of the Day of God."

How do we hasten the coming of the Day of God? Second Peter 3:14 tells us, "Wherefore, beloved, seeing that ye look for such things, be diligent that ye may be found of him in peace, without spot, and blameless." We hasten the Day of God by living godly lives. "And account that the longsuffering of our Lord is salvation" (v. 15). The fact that God is waiting is an evidence of His grace. If God judged the world right now, multitudes would be condemned forever. God is waiting patiently. His patience means salvation for those who trust Him. "The Lord is . . . not willing that any should perish, but that all should come to repentance" (v. 9).

How do you and I hasten the coming of the Day of God? First of all, by living godly lives and keeping our light shining as a witness for Him. Second, by sharing the message of salvation with others. The Lord Jesus is calling out a people for His name. When He has completed His Church, then He will return. By our walk and our witness, we can hasten God's kingdom. If I pray, "Thy kingdom come," but I'm not living a godly life, I'm a hypocrite. If I pray, "Thy kingdom come," but I'm not seeking to win others, I'm not being faithful to God. I'm a hypocrite. So this second responsibility of hastening God's kingdom is very important.

Are the requests that we bring to God going to hasten the coming of His kingdom to earth? If God answers the requests on your prayer list, will it help to hasten the coming of the Lord? Our first responsibility is to honor God's name. Every prayer request ought to do that. Our second responsibility is to hasten God's kingdom. We are looking toward the future—"Thy kingdom come."

Obey God's Will

The third responsibility is to accomplish God's will: "Thy will be done in earth, as it is in heaven" (Matt. 6:10). Prayer has to do with the will of God. I have often quoted Phillips Brooks, who said, "The

131

purpose of prayer is not to get man's will done in heaven, but to get God's will done on earth." First John 5:14,15 makes this very clear. "And this is the confidence that we have in him, that, if we ask any thing according to his will, he heareth us; and if we know that he hear us, whatever we ask, we know that we have the petitions that we desired of him." Prayer is not telling God what to do. Prayer is finding out what God wants to do and then asking Him to do it. "Thy will be done in earth, as it is in heaven."

If we are going to pray in God's will, we have to know the Word of God. The will of God is revealed in the Word of God. We must know the promises, the precepts and the principles of the Word. John 15:7 makes it clear that prayer and the Word go together.

Second, we know God's will when we know God's character. The better a child knows his father, the better that child knows what his father wants to give. Our children knew that they could never come and ask us for anything that would hurt them or that would be evil or worldly. They never bothered to ask for those things because they knew we would never grant them. When you know the character of God because you have studied the Word of God, then you know how to pray. You know what God wants to give.

I think we must also depend on the leading of the Holy Spirit of God. At times in my life the Spirit of God impressed upon my heart a certain prayer request. I didn't understand why at the time. Later on, I usually found out why that burden was on my heart. Jude 1:20 tells us we should pray in the Holy Spirit. Romans 8:26 tells us that the Holy Spirit intercedes for us with groanings that cannot be uttered.

Jesus said in John 4:34, "My food is to do the will of him that sent me, and to finish his work." The will of God accomplishes the work of God, and God's will is nourishment for us. It feeds us. What food is to your body, the will of God should be to your soul. Food gives you strength and satisfaction. You and I should so enjoy the will of God that, as we pray, we delight in His will.

Our Lord Jesus said in John 5:30, "I can of mine own self do nothing. As I hear, I judge; and my judgment is just, because I seek not mine own will, but the will of the Father who hath sent me." That's a good example for us to follow—to do the will of God, to seek the will of God, to try to please God in all things.

Here, then, are three responsibilities that we share; and prayer helps us to fulfill these responsibilities. When you come to the Lord with your prayer requests, ask yourself, *If God granted these requests, would the answers honor His name? If God granted these requests, would it hasten the coming of the Lord Jesus Christ and the establishment of God's kingdom? If God gave me these requests, would it mean His will would be done on earth?*

When our Lord prayed in the garden, He prayed, "Father, if it be possible, let this cup pass from me;

133

nevertheless, not as I will, but as thou wilt" (Matt. 26:39). That is the only way to pray. I have lived long enough to be thankful for *unanswered* prayer. I am glad that God did not give me some of the things I thought I needed. Something happens when churches pray—*if* their prayers honor God's name, hasten God's kingdom and obey God's will.

Chapter 15

The Model Prayer—Requests

Three essentials for effective praying are given to us in the Lord's Prayer. The first is *relationship:* "Our Father, who art in heaven" (Matt. 6:9). I must have a right relationship with my fellow Christians and with the Lord. Relationship leads to *responsibility:* "Hallowed be thy name. Thy kingdom come. Thy will be done in earth, as it is in heaven" (vv. 9,10). Prayer involves the responsibility of glorifying God's name, hastening the coming of His kingdom and accomplishing His will on earth.

Too often we think of praying as simply asking for *things.* But true prayer also involves relationship. If prayer does not draw me closer to my fellow believers and closer to my Father, it is not true spiritual praying. Prayer also involves responsibility. We don't pray for *God* to do something for us. *We* must be available to God to be part of the answer. If I am praying for something to happen in my church or my community but I am unwilling to be part of that answer, my praying is not going to be very effective.

Moses prayed for years that God would deliver the people of Israel when they were in Egypt, and God called Moses to help answer that prayer.

Nehemiah was burdened about the needs of his people in Jerusalem. The gates had been burned, and the walls had been torn down. Nehemiah prayed, and God used him to be a part of that answer.

When God hears us pray, He looks at our hearts and asks, "Are you really sincere? Do you really mean that?" We pray about the financial needs of missionaries, but are we willing to give? We pray about backslidden Christians, but are we loving them and helping to restore them? Prayer involves relationship and responsibility before we come with requests.

Three basic requests are given to us in the Lord's Prayer: "Give us this day our daily bread. And forgive us our debts, as we forgive our debtors. And lead us not into temptation, but deliver us from evil. For thine is the kingdom, and the power, and the glory, forever. Amen" (Matt. 6:11-13).

For Daily Needs

The first request is for our daily needs. God is concerned about the material things of life. So far in the Lord's Prayer, we have not mentioned anything of a material nature. But now we come to the nitty-gritty everyday needs of life. Our Father in heaven is concerned about our daily needs.

Keep in mind that these were *Jewish* men who were learning this prayer. Immediately they would think of the Israelites in the wilderness. When they were hungry in the wilderness, God said, "I will supply bread for you." Early every morning the dew would fall in the camp, and then the manna would fall (see Ex. 16). That manna was a sweet little wafer that sustained them physically throughout their wilderness march.

When Jesus said, "Give us this day our daily bread" (Matt. 6:11), His apostles would have thought immediately of God's supplying the manna from heaven, morning after morning. However, God is not doing that today. When the Israelites were about to enter the Promised Land, the manna ceased and they began to eat the grain that was provided for them.

I hope you never consider your food to be anything less than a miracle. I know we can go to the store and buy it, but God gives us the strength to earn money so that we can purchase our daily bread. When you stop to think of all the miracles that have to take place between the grain of wheat planted in the soil and the loaf of bread that you pick up in the store, it certainly is awesome. Our God is still supplying our every need. Philippians 4:19 makes that very clear: "But my God shall supply all your need according to his riches in glory by Christ Jesus."

In the Lord's Prayer we are taught to pray for the things we need. Someone has well said that God provides our *needs* but not our *greeds*. I think that sometimes our praying becomes rather selfish. Sometimes we don't even know *what* we need! In one of His parables, our Lord said that no father would give his son a stone if the boy begged for bread (see Luke 11:11-13). If the boy asked for an egg, the father would not give him a scorpion. We who are parents will give our children those things that are best for them. The tragedy is that sometimes we Christians don't know *what* we need. We ask for stones and think we are asking for bread. We ask for scorpions when we need eggs. The Father in heaven knows what is best for us.

Our Lord tells us to pray for things a day at a time. That doesn't mean it is wrong to save or to store things up. But it is wrong to try to live two days at a time. "Give us this day [day by day] our daily bread" (Matt. 6:11). We can lay things up for the future; nothing is wrong with that. David stored up the wealth that was needed for the building of the temple. Paul visited the Gentile churches, taking up a collection for the saints in Jerusalem. Nothing is wrong with churches or individuals laying things up for the future; but it is wrong to hoard, for hoarding usually means selfishness and waste. We can ask God to supply our material needs as we require them. This doesn't mean an angel is going to feed us the way he did Elijah. This doesn't mean manna will fall from heaven. It may mean God will just lead you to the right job or that God will give you the strength to do the work that needs to be done. "Give us this day our daily bread."

For Forgiveness

The second request is for forgiveness. We go from "give us" to "forgive us." "Forgive us our debts, as we forgive our debtors" (Matt. 6:12). Sin is pictured in many different ways in the Bible. It is

138

pictured as dirt: "Wash me, and I shall be whiter than snow" (Ps. 51:7). It is pictured as disease. Leprosy, for example, is used as an illustration of sin. Sin is pictured as darkness and as a dungeon where prisoners are confined. Sin is also compared to death: "And you hath he made alive, who were dead in trespasses and sins" (Eph. 2:1).

But in the Lord's Prayer Jesus selected debt as a picture of sin: "Forgive us our debts, as we forgive our debtors" (Matt. 6:12). Sin is a debt. All of us have an obligation to God. God has met our every need. God is holy. God laid down His Law. God had every right to give His Law, and you and I must confess that we are spiritually bankrupt. We are debtors, and we cannot pay! The tragedy is that so many people don't realize how spiritually bankrupt they are! They think they are "rich, and increased with goods, and have need of nothing" when all the while they are "wretched, and miserable, and poor, and blind, and naked" (Rev. 3:17). The Lord looks upon sinners and says, "You are broke. You are bankrupt." And even after we are saved, we realize how much we need Him and how often we need to ask Him for forgiveness.

Sometimes we sin against the Lord and don't even know it. David prayed to be cleansed from secret faults (see Ps. 19:12). These were not sins that he was committing that he didn't think God knew about. They were sins David himself did not know he had committed. Sometimes we sin and don't even realize we have broken God's Law or offended God's people. This is why our Lord gave

139

us the instruction in Matthew 18 that if a brother has offended us, we must go to him and forgive him. Don't go around carrying a grudge. Go tell him about it.

The Bible mentions two different kinds of forgiveness. There is that initial forgiveness that we receive at salvation. Through faith in Jesus Christ, we receive, once and for all, forgiveness for all of our sins. However, there is also *family* forgiveness. Some confused Christians say, "If you've been forgiven once and for all through faith in Jesus Christ, you never again have to ask Christ to forgive you." I don't believe that at all. I believe we need to come before God day by day and say, "Forgive me. I made promises, Lord, and didn't keep them. I did something I wasn't supposed to do."

We must never look at forgiveness as an option. We must never say, "I can go ahead and disobey God and then ask Him to forgive me." If you take that attitude, God will discipline you. Deliberate rebellion against God is serious. Many times we falter and fail in thought and word and deed. We aren't all that God wants us to be, and so we have to ask for forgiveness.

Once again, this request would have been familiar to Jewish people—"Forgive us our debts, as we forgive our debtors" (6:12). Once every 50 years, during the year of Jubilee, all debts were cancelled. So when our Lord said, "Forgive us our debts, as we forgive our debtors," He was talking about something the Jews understood. He was not saying that we must forgive others or else God will not forgive us. He was not saying that we *earn* our forgiveness. He simply taught that if we don't have a heart of repentance so that we forgive others, then our heart is not prepared to ask God for His forgiveness.

The parable of the man who would not forgive the little debt is an illustration of this (see 18:23-35). The king had forgiven him millions of dollars, and yet the servant could not forgive his fellow worker the very small debt that was owed him. I need to pray regularly, "O God, forgive me."

For Guidance

We have the right to pray about daily bread. We have the right to pray about forgiveness. We can also pray about guidance: "Lead us not into temptation, but deliver us from evil [the Evil One]" (Matt. 6:13). God doesn't lead anyone into temptation in the sense of forcing him to be confronted by sin. In James 1 we are told very clearly that God cannot be tempted and that God will not tempt people. What does this request mean? Sometimes you and I become proud and overconfident. That is when we need to pray, "Father, guide me today. Don't let me get myself into a situation where I am tempting myself or I am tempting You." "Lead us not into temptation" simply means "Keep me alert. Keep me aware of the fact that the Wicked One is around and that he wants to trip me up."

Our Lord said in John 17:15, "I pray not that thou shouldest take them out of the world, but that thou shouldest keep them from the evil [the Evil One]." Our Lord said to His disciples, "Watch and pray, that ye enter not into temptation; the spirit indeed is willing, but the flesh is weak" (Matt. 26:41). You and I must be very careful when we feel strong, when we feel confident. That is when we must pray, "Father, help me. I'm liable to walk right into temptation." Satan knows when you and I are overconfident. Paul warned in I Corinthians 10:12, "Let him that thinketh he standeth take heed lest he fall." We are in danger of walking blindly into the sphere of evil and permitting Satan to tempt us. This is what Peter did when he sat by the fire and denied Christ.

For example, when we pray, "Deliver us from evil" (Matt. 6:13), this covers many areas in our lives. Hebrews 10:22 talks about an *evil conscience*. Have you ever asked God to deliver you from an evil conscience? Hebrews 3:12 warns about *an evil heart of unbelief*. Doubt is not the same as unbelief. Doubt is a matter of the mind. When we doubt God, we just can't figure out what He is doing. God is very sympathetic with doubt, but unbelief is an act of the will: "I *will not* believe!" Hebrews 3:12 tells us that unbelief comes from an evil heart and is a wicked sin. Unbelief makes God a liar. It exalts man and makes him the judge of God. Have you ever asked God to deliver you from an evil heart of unbelief?

First Corinthians 15:33 informs us, "Evil company corrupts good morals." Or in today's language, "Bad company ruins good habits or good character." Have you ever asked God to deliver you from evil company? Galatians 1:4 tells us that Jesus died so that we might be delivered from "this present evil age." Some Christians are worldly. If I pray every day, "God, deliver me from evil," then God can deliver me from this present evil world. Ephesians 4:31 warns us about *evil speaking*. How we all need to be delivered from a gossiping tongue! First Thessalonians 5:22 warns us about *all appearance of evil:* "Abstain from all appearance of evil." Because there is so much evil in the world, we need to pray daily, "Lead us not into temptation, but deliver us from evil" (Matt. 6:13). What is the result of all of this? "Thine is the kingdom" (v. 13). God is the Lord; He's the king. He rules over all. "Thine is . . . the power" (v. 13). As a result, "Thine is . . . the glory, forever" (v. 13). I like that word "forever." When you and I are praying at the throne of grace, we are part of eternity. When you and I come to God in prayer, in the name of the Lord Jesus, we are a part of that which is eternal.

Relationship involves responsibility, and responsibility gives us the privilege of request. God will meet our daily needs. He will forgive us. He will guide us and protect us as we obey Him.

A Personal and Practical Postscript

If you have been helped by this book, you may want to share it with others in your church. You also may want to start encouraging others to pray. It would be wonderful if prayer groups would start to spring up all over the world! God promises to bless when His people humble themselves and pray (see II Chron. 7:14).

If you would like additional materials to help you in your prayer life or your personal or family devotions, feel free to write us. Perhaps you would like to become a Back to the Bible Prayer Partner. We will count it a great privilege to send you information. Thousands of Prayer Partners around the world share in the blessing of praying systematically for God's work.

Finally, we would enjoy hearing about the answers to prayer God gives to you and your friends. And if we at the Broadcast can share in your prayer burdens, please write to us. All requests are kept in strictest confidence.

Thank you!

Warren W. Wiersbe
Back to the Bible Broadcast
Box 82808
Lincoln, Nebraska 68501